# THE POET'S CRAFT

Grade 11/12

Front list    2002

# THE POET'S CRAFT

R.J. Ireland

HARCOURT BRACE JOVANOVICH, CANADA

Canadian Cataloguing in Publication Data

Main entry under title:
The Poet's Craft

For high school students.
Includes index.
ISBN 0-7747-1215-5

1. Poetry—Collections. I. Ireland, Robert J., 1936-

PN6101.P62 1984      C821'.008      C84-098772-2

6 7 8 9 10  D  96 95 94 93 92

Printed in Canada

Composition by CompuScreen Typesetting Ltd.

Design by Michael van Elsen Design Inc.

Cover photograph by Ellie Forrest

ISBN: 0-7747-1215-5

# Table of Contents

# Note to the Reader

Each time you read a poem, you can get something different from it. You should not feel that you must get a poem's full meaning and impact from one reading. The poet's language is usually different from the language you use every day. More importantly, the poet's experience is different from yours. Expect to read a poem more than once.

After a first reading, think about your reactions to the poem, whatever they may be. Don't try to think about how you *should* react. Just honestly think about how you *have* reacted. On a second reading, try to see what caused that reaction. Look for the thought of the poem. Notice the punctuation, and use it as a guide to find the sentences in the poem. It is often helpful to write a paraphrase° of the poem—a summary of what the poem says.

Your first reading should be fairly quick. Do not stop to look up words or to figure out difficult parts. It might take you two or three quick readings to get the general sense of the poem. Then make a couple of slower readings to figure out the thought. Several quick readings are better than one or two slow ones; and you should try reading the poem aloud, either in class or quietly to yourself, at least once.

When you read a poem you must make the meaning. Don't wait for the meaning to jump off the page into your head. There must be an active interaction between the words on the page and the meanings and understandings in your head. As you read, relate the ideas in the poem to your own experiences. That is what interpreting a poem means. Interpretation is the interaction of the reader and the poem.

# PART I

# WHAT ARE POEMS ABOUT?

# Introduction

Poems° can be about anything in the human mind. We experience events; we meet people; we go places; we feel emotions; we have thoughts—any of these can be the subject matter for a poem. In this first section of *The Poet's Craft*, the poems are grouped under six headings that apply to many human experiences: *Life and Death*; *Love and Loneliness*; *War and Hope*; *People and Places*; *Nature and Invention*; and, finally, *Anything and Everything*. Other topics° could have been chosen, but these will allow for some interesting explorations.

Because poetry can be composed about anything which the human mind can imagine, poems have long been a way for people to express themselves. Our topics will enable us to share what other people have thought and felt about many things that are also of concern to us.

There's one other thing you should consider at this time. Poems are not just personal statements about a topic. They are also a special use of language. They express more than the words say. You will find the full meaning of a poem by letting yourself be open to the complete range of experiences the poem presents.

Each poem makes a statement (its *theme*) about something (its *topic*). The *sense* of the poem is one kind of meaning; so are *feeling*, *tone*, and *intention*. These various kinds of meanings become clear as you sense the *structure* and the *unity* of the poem.

These aren't terms to memorize. They simply describe some of the kinds of meaning you will come to notice more and more automatically as you read more poetry. So, each time a new topic is introduced in this part of the book, there is also a discussion of one or more of these kinds of meaning.

# 1 LIFE AND DEATH

## Exploring Meaning: Theme and Topic

In its simplest terms, a poem is a statement about something:
- What the poem is about is the topic° (or subject) of the poem.
- What the poem says *about the topic* is the theme° of the poem.

Following are two groups of poems. The topic of the first group of poems is "Life." The topic of the second group is "Death." When you can summarize what one of these poems says about life or death, you will have made a decision about the theme of that poem. With additional readings your interpretation may well change. The best statements of theme can be supported by reference to all the important aspects of a poem. But you will learn about these gradually. Right now, concentrate on getting the general sense of these poems about life and death.

## Life

What are your opinions on these questions?
- What is life?
- Is there any life after our present one?
- What makes for a happy life?

Questions like these have been raised for thousands of years. Answers have been suggested in songs, dances, stories, performances, paintings, sculpture, and, of course, in poetry. What do these poets say about life?

## CHRONOLOGY

I was born senile and gigantic
my wrinkles charting
in pink the heights and ruts, events
of all possible experience.

At 6 I was sly as a weasel,                                                  5
adroit at smiling and hiding,
slippery-fingered, greasy with guile.

At 12, instructed
by the comicbooks already
latent in my head, I was bored with horror.                                 10

At 16 I was pragmatic,
armoured with wry lipstick;
I was invulnerable,
I wore my hair like a helmet.

But by 20 I had begun                                                       15
to shed knowledge like petals
or scales; and today I discovered
that I have been living backwards.

Time wears me down like water.
The engraved lines of my features                                           20
are being slowly expunged.

I will have to pretend:
the snail knows
thin skin is no protection;

though I can't go on                                                        25
indefinitely. At 50 they will peel
my face away like a nylon stocking

uncovering such incredible blank
innocence, that even mirrors
accustomed to grotesques                                                    30
will be astounded.

---

*Chronology*: a listing of events in the order in which they happened.
*latent* (l.10): hidden; capable of later development.
*pragmatic* (l.11): practical, business-like.
*expunged* (l.21): blotted out; erased.
*grotesques* (l.30): in painting or sculpture, designs and figures of persons or
  animals combined in fantastic, unnatural ways; also clowns or freaks.

---

I will be unshelled, I will be
of no use to that city
and like a horse with a broken back
I will have to be taken out and shot.                35

MARGARET ATWOOD (b. 1939)


## GREETINGS FROM THE
## INCREDIBLE SHRINKING WOMAN

it's not that
i'm getting smaller
(i thought so at first)
but that the continent's

expanding, stretching                                5
like silly putty
or like a movie
seen in a dream

landmarks, even back fences,
recede; where i am                                   10
is always empty

i used to see myself
at the land's edge
waiting maybe to be
flicked off,                                         15
to thrash like a fish
in the saltchuck

now it's miles from
my house even
to the Fraser River                                  20
which is immense,
swollen like throat-veins

and the landscape continues
to pull out
while i do nothing                                   25

just by standing
here, i'm dwindling

---

*saltchuck* (l.17): a west coast term for the sea; salt water.

to a dot.
(actually it's that
i'm finally learning
perspective)                                            30

PAT LOWTHER (1935-1975)


## PREPAREDNESS

For all your days prepare,
   And meet them ever alike:
When you are the anvil, bear—
   When you are the hammer, strike.

EDWIN MARKHAM (1852-1940)


## ON HIS BLINDNESS

When I consider how my light is spent,
   Ere half my days, in this dark world and wide,
   And that one talent which is death to hide,
   Lodg'd with me useless, though my soul more bent
To serve therewith my Maker, and present          5
   My true account, lest he returning chide,
   "Doth God exact day-labour, light denied?"
   I fondly ask. But Patience, to prevent
That murmur, soon replies, "God doth not need
   Either man's work or his own gifts; who best
   Bear his mild yoke, they serve him best; his state
Is kingly; thousands at his bidding speed
   And post o'er land and ocean without rest:
   They also serve who only stand and wait."

JOHN MILTON (1608-1674)

---

*Preparedness*: this poem is an epigram°.
*anvil* (l.4): iron or steel block used by a blacksmith for shaping metals.

---

*On His Blindness*: Milton became blind when he was 44 years old.
*spent* (l.1): used up.
*ere* (l.2): before.
*that one talent* (l.3): his talent for writing.
*more bent* (l.4): more inclined.
*chide* (l.6): scold.

## THE ALBERTA HOMESTEADER

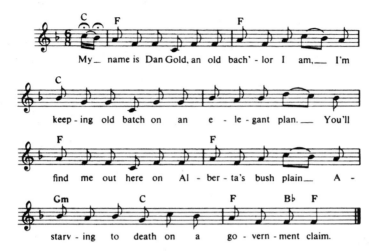

My＿ name is Dan Gold, an old bach' - lor I am,＿ I'm keep - ing old batch on an e - le - gant plan.＿ You'll find me out here on Al - ber - ta's bush plain＿ A - starv - ing to death on a go - vern - ment claim.

1. My name is Dan Gold, an old bach'lor I am,
   I'm keeping old batch on an elegant plan.
   You'll find me out here on Alberta's bush plain
   A-starving to death on a government claim.

2. So come to Alberta, there's room for you all,                    5
   Where the wind never ceases and the rain always falls,
   Where the sun always sets and there it remains
   Till we get frozen out on our government claims.

3. My house it is built of the natural soil,
   My walls are erected according to Hoyle,                         10
   My roof has no pitch, it is level and plain,
   And I always get wet when it happens to rain.

4. My clothes are all ragged, my language is rough,
   My bread is case-hardened and solid and tough,

---

*The Alberta Homesteader*: a homestead was a government grant of land
   given to a settler who agreed to remain on it for a certain period of time.
*according to Hoyle* (l.10): by the highest authority; from Edmond Hoyle
   who wrote several books on the strategy and rules of card and other
   games.
*case-hardened* (l.14): hardened on the surface, e.g. as iron is by partial
   cementation; stale.

My dishes are scattered all over the room,  15
My floor gets afraid at the sight of a broom.

5. How happy I feel when I roll into bed:
The rattlesnake rattles a tune at my head,
The little mosquito devoid of all fear
Crawls over my face and into my ear.  20

6. The little bedbug so cheerful and bright,
It keeps me up laughing two-thirds of the night,
And the smart little flea with tacks in his toes
Crawls up through my whiskers and tickles my nose.

7. You may try to raise wheat, you may try to raise rye.  25
You may stay there and live, you may stay there and die,
But as for myself, I'll no longer remain
A-starving to death on a government claim.

8. So farewell to Alberta, farewell to the west,
It's backwards I'll go to the girl I love best.  30
I'll go back to the east and get me a wife
And never eat cornbread the rest of my life.

AUTHOR UNKNOWN


## THE BANKS OF NEWFOUNDLAND

1. Oh, ye may bless your happy lots, all ye who dwell on
      shore,
   For it's little ye know of the hardships that we poor
      seamen [b]ore.
   It's little ye know of the hardships that we were forced
      to stand
   For fourteen days and fifteen nights on the banks of
      Newfoundland.

2. Our ship she sailed through frost and snow from the
      day we left Quebec,  5
   And if we had not walked about we'd have frozen to
      the deck,
   But we being true-born sailormen as ever a ship had
      manned,
   Our captain doubled our grog each day on the banks of
      Newfoundland.

---

*grog* (l.8): a sailor's daily portion of alcohol, usually rum.

3. There never was a ship, my boys, that sailed the
   western sea
   But the billowy waves came rolling in and bent them
   into staves.                                                    10
   Our ship being built of unseasoned wood and could
   but little stand,
   The hurricane it met us there on the banks of
   Newfoundland.

4. We fasted for three days and nights, our provisions
   giving out.
   On the morning of the fourth day, we cast our lots about.
   The lot it fell on the captain's son; thinking relief at
   hand,                                                          15
   We spared him for another night on the banks of
   Newfoundland.

5. On the morning of the fifth day no vessel did appear.
   We gave to him another hour to offer up a prayer,
   But Providence to us proved kind, kept blood from
   every hand,
   For an English vessel hove in sight on the banks of
   Newfoundland.                                                  20

6. We hoisted aloft our signal; they bore down on us
   straightway.
   When they saw our pitiful condition, they began to
   weep and pray.
   Five hundred souls we had on board the day we left
   the land:
   There's now alive but seventy-five on the banks of
   Newfoundland.

7. They took us off of the wreck, my boys; we were more
   like ghosts than men.                                         25
   They fed us and they clothed us and brought us back
   again.
   They fed us and they clothed us and brought us safe to
   land,
   While the billowy waves roll o'er their graves on the
   banks of Newfound*land*.

AUTHOR UNKNOWN

---

*staves* (l.10): curved pieces of wood as those used in a barrel.
*Providence* (l.19): God; God's help.

---

## OUR DAILY DEATH

Sleep under my shoulder
like a deer below a hill

No one understands the world
Only how it evolves without us
All we can do is imagine                                        5
the world continues while we sleep
Though we don't believe it

Someone is awake and watching
so the stars don't move to another heaven
while we sleep                                                  10

And while we sleep the world waits
till morning, like a thug in an alley

Full of hatred, guilt and self pity
that we arm for in our dreams

So sleep beneath my shoulder                                    15
while I watch imagined stars

I believe in nothing I can't touch
I believe in you, while you are here

SID MARTY (b. 1944)

# Death

Does death worry you? Why or why not?
- What is death?
- What remains after it?
- How should we prepare for it?

As many questions have been asked about death as about life, for death is the inescapable fate of every living thing. What do these poets say about it?

## MY BROTHER DYING

As he looks up at us
With his fear-glazed eyes,
Does he picture us buzzards
Circling round his bed,
Waiting patiently                                          5
For his death and his bones?

No: just his mother, his brother,
Who could do nothing for him
When he sat with the living,
And can do nothing now                                     10
As he crawls toward death.

RAYMOND SOUSTER (b. 1921)

## DEATH BE NOT PROUD

Death, be not proud, though some have called thee
Mighty and dreadful, for thou art not so,
For those whom thou think'st thou dost overthrow
Die not, poor death, nor yet canst thou kill me.
From rest and sleep, which but thy pictures be,            5
Much pleasure, then from thee, much more must flow,
And soonest our best men with thee do go,
Rest of their bones and soul's delivery.
Thou art slave to fate, chance, kings, and desperate men,
And dost with poison, war, and sickness dwell,             10

---

*Much pleasure* (l.6): a word such as "follows" or "comes" must be understood. So the thought in lines 5 and 6 is "Much pleasure comes from rest and sleep, which are images of you."

And poppy or charms can make us sleep as well,
And better than thy stroke; why swell'st thou then?
One short sleep past, we wake eternally,
And death shall be no more; death, thou shalt die.

JOHN DONNE (1572-1631)


## OZYMANDIAS

I met a traveler from an antique land
Who said: "Two vast and trunkless legs of stone
Stand in the desert. Near them, on the sand,
Half sunk, a shattered visage lies, whose frown,
And wrinkled lip, and sneer of cold command,                    5
Tell that its sculptor well those passions read
Which yet survive, stamped on these lifeless things,
The hand that mocked them, and the heart that fed:
And on the pedestal these words appear:
'My name is Ozymandias, king of kings:                          10
Look on my works, ye Mighty, and despair!'
Nothing beside remains. Round the decay
Of that colossal wreck, boundless and bare
The lone and level sands stretch far away."

PERCY BYSSHE SHELLEY (1792-1822)

---

*poppy* (l.11): opium.
*Why swell'st thou?* (l.12): Why do you swell with pride?

---

*Ozymandias*: according to a Greek historian of the first century B.C. the
  statue of Ozymandias was the largest in Egypt.
*visage* (l.4): face.
*The hand that mocked them* (l.8): the hand of the sculptor who reproduced
  the passions.
*the heart that fed* (l.8): the heart of Ozymandias from which the passions
  came.

## THE UNKNOWN CITIZEN
*(To JS/07/M/378 This Marble Monument is Erected
by the State)*

He was found by the Bureau of Statistics to be
One against whom there was no official complaint,
And all the reports on his conduct agree
That, in the modern sense of an old-fashioned word, he
    was a saint,
For in everything he did he served the Greater
    Community.          5
Except for the War till the day he retired
He worked in a factory and never got fired,
But satisfied his employers, Fudge Motors Inc.
Yet he wasn't a scab or odd in his views,
For his Union reports that he paid his dues,      10
(Our report on his Union shows it was sound)
And our Social Psychology workers found
That he was popular with his mates and liked a drink.
The Press are convinced that he bought a paper every day
And that his reactions to advertisements were normal in
    every way.      15
Policies taken out in his name prove that he was fully
    insured,
And his Health-card shows he was once in hospital but
    left it cured.
Both Producers Research and High-Grade Living declare
He was fully sensible to the advantages of the Installment
    Plan
And had everything necessary to the Modern Man,    20
A phonograph, a radio, a car and a frigidaire.
Our researchers into Public Opinion are content
That he held the proper opinions for the time of year;
When there was peace, he was for peace; when there was
    war, he went.
He was married and added five children to the population, 25

---

*The Unknown Citizen*: in many cemeteries there is a monument to the
    unknown soldier, an unidentified soldier who was killed in battle, who is
    buried there and is honored as the representative of all the unidentified
    war dead of his or her country.
*To JS/07/M/378 . . .*: this epitaph forms an important part of the poem and
    should be read as carefully as the rest of it.
*scab* (l.9): strike-breaker.

Which our Eugenist says was the right number for a
    parent of his generation,
And our teachers report that he never interfered with their
    education.
Was he free? Was he happy? The question is absurd:
Had anything been wrong, we should certainly have heard.

W.H. AUDEN (1907-1973)


## L'ENVOI: IN BEECHWOOD CEMETERY

Beneath the coverlet
    of October leaves
all beginnings and ends.

    I no longer scorn
funerals, having learned                      5
    only that it's later

than I thought. No comfort
    love or books;
of no stellar consequence

    other alloys of atoms                 10
or amino-acids. The stars
    serve as tapers

for cosmic burial-rites,
    will themselves
sputter out. And the perfect          15

    peace of nothingness
will drift as surely
    as tranquilly,

as finally as these leaves
    now settle                      20
on the universal tomb:

---

L'envoi: a postscript, usually to a prose work and expressing a moral.
stellar (l.9): relating to the stars; in this context, very important.
amino-acids (l.11): the constituents of protein molecules; used in the body's
    cells for growth, repair and maintenance.
tapers (l.12): candles.

as beautiful
and as utterly useless
as a poem.

HARRY HOWITH (b. 1934)

## THE CHANCE-TAKING DEAD

A field of Ontario Quaker graves
very old
no headstones
nothing showing where the graves are

An acre or more of grassland                      5
intense with devout dead
who entered underground
on their own plan to lie unknown

In this uneven field
some mounds of longer grass               10
two dying elms
a few protruding glacial stones

No new graves
Congregation gone
Religion gone                                        15
I stare at the chance-taking dead

R.G. EVERSON (b. 1903)

## IF I SHOULD DIE TO-NIGHT

If I should die to-night
And you should come to my cold corpse and say,
Weeping and heartsick o'er my lifeless clay—
    If I should die to-night,
And you should come in deepest grief and woe—        5
And say: "Here's that ten dollars that I owe,"
    I might arise in my large white cravat
    And say, "What's that?"

    If I should die to-night
And you should come to my cold corpse and kneel,        10
Clasping my bier to show the grief you feel,
    I say, if I should die to-night
And you should come to me, and there and then

*cravat* (l.7): necktie.

Just even hint 'bout paying me that ten,
I might arise the while,
But I'd drop dead again.

BEN KING

---

# LIFE AND DEATH: QUESTIONS

## A. Life

### Chronology (p. 4)

1. Why is the first line surprising? In what way *is* a baby a giant?
2. This poem divides into two parts. It also changes tenses. Where are the shifts in thought?
3. Line 17 is the exact middle of the poem, and perhaps coincidentally it is right there that the speaker stops counting. What do you think is the significance of this?
4. In the final stanza°, how seriously did you take the speaker?
5. Decide the poem's theme.

### Greetings from the Incredible Shrinking Woman (p. 5)

1. How does the speaker see her life? Compare the first stanza of this poem with the first stanza of *Chronology* on page 4.
2. Look for lines and phrases in the poem which give a sense of how the speaker feels about the way her life is going.
3. State in your own words the thought expressed in the final parentheses.
4. What is your opinion of this statement about life? That is, what is your opinion of the theme of the poem?

### Preparedness (p. 6)

1. Paraphrase° the last two lines of the poem.
2. How is this poem different from the previous poems about life?
3. Compare the theme of this poem with the themes of the previous two poems. In which poem was the theme most clearly stated?

---

*bier* (l.11): stand on which the coffin is placed.

**On His Blindness (p. 6)**

1. Notice that the first sentence does not end until the middle of line 8. Reread that sentence and state its meaning in your own words.
2. The last six and one half lines are also one sentence. State the meaning of that sentence in your own words.
3. What is the theme of the poem? Where is the theme stated?
4. Is the poem hopeful and optimistic, or is it pessimistic? Give reasons for your opinion.

**The Alberta Homesteader (p. 8)**

1. What does the song reveal about the homesteader's life?
2. What feeling is expressed by the song? How do you account for this feeling?
3. In what way is the song ironic°?
4. Is there a theme to this song? If so, what is it? If not, what do you think was the author's purpose in writing the song?

**The Banks of Newfoundland (p. 9)**

1. How is the feeling expressed by this song different from that expressed in *The Alberta Homesteader*?
2. How are the two songs similar?
3. Songs such as these are still popular. What might account for this popularity?

**Our Daily Death (p. 11)**

1. Briefly summarize the thought expressed in this poem.
2. Why do you think the poet chose the simile°, "like a thug in an alley" to describe how the world waits?
3. How do you think the speaker feels about life? Support your opinion with references to the poem.

---

# B. Death

**My Brother Dying (p. 13)**

1. What feeling does the poem create in you? Why?
2. What view of death is presented?
3. Compare this poem with some of the others in this group. How is it different in feeling, in theme and in structure?
4. Do you think this poem makes an effective statement of the theme? Give reasons for your answer.

## Death Be Not Proud (p. 13)

1. This poem is a sonnet°. Sonnets vary somewhat in structure, but this one follows a 4-4-4-2 line pattern.
   a. The first four lines form an introduction. What statement do they make?
   b. The next four lines give a reason for the conclusions in line 4. What "proof" is given?
   c. The next four lines continue to mock Death. How is Death made to seem powerless?
   d. What final proof or belief is stated in the last two lines?
2. This poem is presented as though one person were speaking to another. What is gained by having Death appear as a person?
3. Is the argument presented in this poem effective and convincing?

## Ozymandias (p. 14)

1. This poem, like Donne's *Death Be Not Proud*, is a sonnet°, but the structure of this poem is 8-6.
   a. What picture and thought are presented in the first eight lines?
   b. What thought is presented in the last six lines?
2. This poem makes its points by the use of irony°. It shows that superficial appearances are different from the inner realities. What is the theme° of the poem?
3. Of the two poems, *My Brother Dying* (p. 13) and *Death Be Not Proud* (p. 13), to which do you think this one is most similar?

## The Unknown Citizen (p. 15)

1. How does the epitaph help to introduce the theme of the poem?
2. Who might be speaking in the poem?
3. Examine the poem by sentences. What is the topic of each sentence in the poem?
4. What meanings could the word "unknown" in the title have besides the one suggested in the notes?
5. What is the theme of the poem? How is the theme made clear and emphatic?

## L'Envoi: In Beechwood Cemetery (p. 16)

1. This poem has a moral rather than a theme. Because the poem is a "l'envoi", it is important to recognize its moral. State the moral in your own words.
2. In the last three stanzas the speaker compares peace, the leaves and a poem. What similarities does he find among them?

3. What does the cemetery make the poet consider? Why do you think it has this effect on him?

### The Chance-Taking Dead (p. 17)
1. Why does the speaker say the dead have taken chances?
2. Explain the thought expressed in the line, "intense with devout dead".
3. What is the theme of this poem? What is your opinion of the statement the poem makes?
4. Compare this poem to *L'Envoi: In Beechwood Cemetery* (p. 16). In what ways are they similar? How are they different?

### If I Should Die To-Night (p. 17)
1. How does the language in the last four lines of each stanza° change to match the transition in the author's mood from seriousness to humor?
2. Do you think it is in bad taste to make a joke about death? Give reasons for your opinion.
3. Could this poem be making a serious statement about death? What might that statement be?

# 2 LOVE AND LONELINESS

## Exploring Meaning: Sense and Feeling

SENSE° IS the starting point for interpretation. The meaning° of a poem comes in many ways, but to understand a poem, you must first grasp its sense—that is, you must know what the words mean.

The sense of a poem is conveyed in the same way as the sense of a story or an essay—through words and sentences. Although a few poems do not use punctuation, most do; and punctuation is a clue to the sense. When you read these poems the third or fourth time (after one or two quick readings), look for the sentences that make them up. Try to get the sense of each sentence, but try not to forget the way you feel after reading the poem. You might also find it useful to have a dictionary handy, not only to check unfamiliar words but also to see if familiar words could have unusual meanings.

Finding the sense is the first step to a deeper understanding of the poem and to an appreciation of how it creates its effect.

## Love

- What is love?
- What causes it?
- What kinds of love are there?

## SONNET 43: HOW DO I LOVE THEE?

How do I love thee? Let me count the ways.
I love thee to the depth and breadth and height
My soul can reach, when feeling out of sight
For the ends of Being and ideal Grace.
I love thee to the level of everyday's                    5
Most quiet need, by sun and candle-light.
I love thee freely, as men strive for Right;
I love thee purely, as they turn from Praise.
I love thee with the passion put to use
In my old griefs, and with my childhood's faith.          10
I love thee with a love I seemed to lose
With my lost saints—I love thee with the breath,
Smiles, tears, of all my life!—and, if God choose,
I shall but love thee better after death.

ELIZABETH BARRETT BROWNING (1806-1861)


## FIRST PERSON DEMONSTRATIVE

I'd rather
heave half a brick than say
I love you, though I do
I'd rather
crawl in a hole than call you                             5
darling, though you are
I'd rather
wrench off an arm than hug you though
it's what I long to do
I'd rather                                                10
gather a posy of poison ivy than
ask if you love me

so if my
hair doesn't stand on end it's because
I never tease it                                          15

---

*the ends of Being* (l.4): the purpose of life.
*ideal Grace* (l.4): the grace of God; God's inspiration and assistance in
    human life.
*with my lost saints*: (l.12): the faith of her childhood.
*better after death* (l.14): she knew she was close to death when she wrote
    this sonnet.

---

and if my
heart isn't in my mouth it's because
it knows its place
and if I
don't take a bite of your ear it's because                    20
gristle gripes my guts
and if you
miss the message better get new
glasses and read it twice

PHYLLIS GOTLIEB (b. 1926)


## THE PASSIONATE SHEPHERD TO HIS LOVE

Come live with me, and be my love,
And we will all the pleasures prove,
That valleys, groves, hills, and fields,
Woods, or steepy mountain yields.

And we will sit upon the rocks,                              5
Seeing the shepherds feed their flocks,
By shallow rivers, to whose falls
Melodious birds sing madrigals.

And I will make thee beds of roses,
And a thousand fragrant posies,                             10
A cap of flowers, and a kirtle
Embroidered all with leaves of myrtle;

A gown made of the finest wool,
Which from our pretty lambs we pull,
Fair lined slippers for the cold,                           15
With buckles of the purest gold;

A belt of straw and ivy buds,
With coral clasps and amber studs,
And if these pleasures may thee move,
Come live with me, and be my love.                          20

The shepherd swains shall dance and sing

---

*prove* (l.2): experience; try out.
*yields* (l.4): offers; presents.
*madrigals* (l.8): country songs, usually about love.
*kirtle* (l.11): a gown or outer petticoat.
*swains* (l.21): lovers.

For they delight each May-morning.
If these delights thy mind may move,
Then live with me, and be my love.

CHRISTOPHER MARLOWE (1564-1593)


## LOVE UNDER THE REPUBLICANS
## (OR DEMOCRATS)

Come live with me and be my love
And we will all the pleasures prove
Of a marriage conducted with economy
In the Twentieth Century Anno Donomy.
We'll live in a dear little walk-up flat                     5
With practically room to swing a cat
And a potted cactus to give it hauteur
And a bathtub equipped with dark brown water.
We'll eat, without undue discouragement
Foods low in cost but high in nouragement                    10
And quaff with pleasure, while chatting wittily,
The peculiar wine of Little Italy.
We'll remind each other it's smart to be thrifty
And buy our clothes for something-fifty.
We'll stand in line on holidays                              15
For seats at unpopular matinees,
And every Sunday we'll have a lark
And take a walk in Central Park.
And one of these days not too remote
I'll probably up and cut your throat.                        20

OGDEN NASH (1902-1971)


## MEMORY

In the first evenings
when we walked together
spring had taken the city
by the hand.

---

*Anno Donomy* (l.4): Anno Domini (A.D.); Latin for "the year of the lord."
*hauteur* (l.7): snobbish manner.
*nouragement* (l.10): nourishment.
*quaff* (l.11): drink, usually with reference to wine.
*Little Italy* (l.12): an area in New York City.

---

We would walk silent or speaking          5
down a dozen unknown streets
of clustered houses
while the night was soft as lips
upon our skin.

As we walked through the dark,          10
lighted windows
made mysteries, made
a hundred private worlds.

Now in a house
where children sleep
we live within the light
and from our window
see sometimes
the shapes of lovers in the evening streets.

DAVID HELWIG (b. 1938)


## MARRIAGE

After seven years
I've almost succeeded
in freeing my wife
from her ludicrous fear
of electrical storms.          5

Tonight she parted
the curtains to watch
the lightning burst open
like an enormous golden
flower, consume itself, die          10
to the accompaniment
of the sound the sky might
make if it were
solid and could be
cracked open from          15
horizon to zenith.

And I flinched.

---

*ludicrous* (1.4): silly, ridiculous.
*zenith* (1.16): point in the heavens directly overhead; taken as the highest
    point of one's life, career, etc.

After seven years.

That much of her
implanted in me.                                        20

ALDEN NOWLAN (1933-1983)

## LOST JIMMY WHELAN

1. Lonely I strayed by the banks of a river
   Watching the sunbeams as evening drew nigh.
   As onward I rambled I spied a fair damsel,
   She was weeping and wailing with many a sigh,

2. Crying for one who is now lying lonely,            5
   Sighing for one who no mortal could see,
   For the dark rolling waters flow gently around him
   As onward she speeds over young Jimmy's grave.

3. She cries, "Oh, my darling, won't you come to my
       arrums
   And give me fond kisses which ofttimes you gave?    10
   You promised to meet me this evening, my darling,
   So now, lovelie Jimmy, arise from your grave."

4. Slowly he rose from the dark stormy waters,

---

*arrums* (l.9): arms.

A vision of beauty far fairer than sun.
Pink and red were the garments all round him,          15
And unto this fair maid to speak he began,

5. Saying, "Why do you rise me from the re-alms of glory
   Back to this place where I once had to leave?"
   "It was to embrace in your strong loving arrums,
   So now lovelie Jimmy, take me to your grave."          20

6. "Darling," he says, "you are asking a favor
   That no earthly mortal could grant unto thee,
   For death is the debtor that tore us asunder
   And wide is the gulf, love, between you and me.

7. "Hard, hard were the struggles on the cruel
      Mississippi,                                           25
   But encircled around her on every side,
   Thinking of you as we conquered them bravely,
   I was hoping some day for to make you my bride.

8. "But in vain was the hopes that arose in my bosom,
   And nothing, oh nothing, on earth could be saved.       30
   My last dying thoughts were of God and you, darling,
   Till death took me down to the deep silent grave.

9. "One fond embrace, love, and then I must leave you.
   One loving farewell, and then we must part."
   Cold were the arms that encircled around her            35
   And cold was the form that she pressed to her heart.

10. Slowly he rose from the banks of the river.
    Up to the sky he then seemed to go,
    Leaving this fair maid on the banks of the river,
    Sighing and weeping in anger and woe.                  40

11. Throwing herself on the banks of the river,
    Crying as though her poor heart it would break,
    She cried, "Oh, my darling, my lost Jimmy Whelan,
    I'll lie down and die by the side of *your grave.*"

AUTHOR UNKNOWN

---

*re-alms* (l.17): realms, kingdoms (the word is hypenated to make the
pronunciation fit the melody and rhythm of the song).

FEELING° IS another part of the total meaning of a poem. Often when we read a poem we get a certain feeling° even before we fully understand the poem's sense. The value of a poem is in our total experience of it, and an important part of that experience is our feelings or emotions. But, just as we need to go beyond our own meanings of words to find the poet's meanings, we also have to go beyond our own feelings to find the poet's feelings about the topic of the poem. For example, we may read a poem and feel sad because we have experienced loneliness as the person in the poem has. But on further reading, we may find that the speaker° in the poem enjoys the loneliness for some reason.

So, while we react emotionally to a poem, we must, where necessary, make a distinction between the poet's emotion and ours.

# Loneliness

Loneliness, like love, is a common human emotion:
- What is loneliness?
- Is being alone the same as being lonely?
- Are there ways to cheer ourselves up when we are lonely?
- Does loneliness serve any useful purpose?

### SOMEONE WHO USED TO HAVE SOMEONE

There used to be someone
to whom I could say do you
love me and be sure that the
answer would always be yes;
there used to be someone to          5
whom I could telephone and
be sure when the operator
said do you accept the charges
the answer would always be yes;
but now there is no one to ask          10
no one to telephone from the
strangeness of cities in the
lateness of nightness now there
is no one always now no one
no someone no never at all.          15

Can you imagine what it is
like to live in a world where
there is no one now always no

no one and never some some-
one to ask do you love me and                                    20
be sure that the answer would
always be yes? I live in a world
where only the billboards are
always   they're twenty feet tall
and they circle the city they                                    25
coax and caress me they heat
me and cool me they promise and
plead me with color and comfort:
*you can get to sleep with me*
*tonight* (the me being ovaltine)                                30
but who wants to get to sleep
with a cup of ovaltine what
kind of sleep is that for someone who used to have someone
to ask do you love me and                                        35
be sure that the answer
would always be yes?

MIRIAM WADDINGTON (b. 1917)


## ACQUAINTED WITH THE NIGHT

I have been one acquainted with the night.
I have walked out in rain—and back in rain.
I have outwalked the furthest city light.

I have looked down the saddest city lane.
I have passed by the watchman on his beat.                       5
And dropped my eyes, unwilling to explain.

I have stood still and stopped the sound of feet
When far away an interrupted cry
Came over houses from another street,

But not to call me back or say goodbye;                          10
And further still at an unearthly height,
One luminary clock against the sky

Proclaimed the time was neither wrong nor right.
I have been one acquainted with the night.

ROBERT FROST (1874-1963)

---

*luminary* (l.12): a natural-light giving body; here, the moon.

---

## THE FORSAKEN

I

Once in the winter
Out on a lake
In the heart of the northland,
Far from the Fort
And far from the hunters,                                  5
A Chippewa woman
With her sick baby,
Crouched in the last hours
Of a great storm.
Frozen and hungry,                                         10
She fished through the ice
With a line of the twisted
Bark of the cedar,
And a rabbit-bone hook
Polished and barbed;                                       15
Fished with the bare hook
All through the wild day,
Fished and caught nothing;
While the young chieftain
Tugged at her breasts,                                     20
Or slept in the lacings
Of the warm *tikanagan*.
All the lake-surface
Streamed with the hissing
Of millions of iceflakes                                   25
Hurled by the wind;
Behind her the round
Of a lonely island
Roared like a fire
With the voice of the storm                                30
In the deeps of the cedars.
Valiant, unshaken,
She took of her own flesh,
Baited the fish-hook,

---

*Chippewa* (l.6): also "Ojibwa"; adapted from the native term "Otchibway" meaning "those whose moccasins have puckered seams"; Amerindians who occupy land from the Ottawa Valley west to the Prairies.

*tikanagan* (l.22): a device made of reeds and having leather straps used for carrying a child on the mother's back.

Drew in a gray-trout,                                                   35
Drew in his fellows,
Heaped them beside her,
Dead in the snow.
Valiant, unshaken,
She faced the long distance,                                            40
Wolf-haunted and lonely,
Sure of her goal
And the life of her dear one:
Tramped for two days,
On the third in the morning,                                           45
Saw the strong bulk
Of the Fort by the river,
Saw the wood-smoke
Hang soft in the spruces,
Heard the keen yelp                                                    50
Of the ravenous huskies
Fighting for whitefish:
Then she had rest.

                    II
Years and years after,
When she was old and withered,                                        55
When her son was an old man
And his children filled with vigor,
They came in their northern tour on the verge of winter,
To an island in a lonely lake.
There one night they camped, and on the morrow            60
Gathered their kettles and birch-bark
Their rabbit-skin robes and their mink-traps,
Launched their canoes and slunk away through the islands,
Left her alone forever,
Without a word of farewell,                                            65
Because she was old and useless,
Like a paddle broken and warped,
Or a pole that was splintered.
Then, without a sigh,
Valiant, unshaken,                                                    70
She smoothed her dark locks under her kerchief,
Composed her shawl in state,
Then folded her hands ridged with sinews and corded with
    veins,

*keen* (l.50): sharp, piercing, eager.

Folded them across her breasts spent with the nourishing
   of children,
Gazed at the sky past the tops of the cedars,        75
Saw two spangled nights arise out of the twilight,
Saw two days go by filled with the tranquil sunshine,
Saw, without pain, or dread, or even a moment of longing:
Then on the third great night there came thronging and
   thronging
Millions of snowflakes out of a windless cloud;        80
They covered her close with a beautiful crystal shroud,
Covered her deep and silent.
But in the frost of the dawn,
Up from the life below,
Rose a column of breath
Through a tiny cleft in the snow,        85
Fragile, delicately drawn,
Wavering with its own weakness,
In the wilderness a sign of the spirit,
Persisting still in the sight of the sun        90
Till day was done.
Then all light was gathered up by the hand of God and
   hid in His breast,
Then there was born a silence deeper than silence,
Then she had rest.

DUNCAN CAMPBELL SCOTT (1862-1947)


## WABANAKI SONG

Now I am left on this lonely island to die—
No one to hear the sound of my voice.
Who will bury me when I die?
Who will sing my death-song for me?
My false friends leave me here to die alone;        5
Like a wild beast, I am left on this island to die.
I wish the wind spirit would carry my cry to my love!
My love is as swift as the deer; he would speed through
   the forest to find me;

*Wabanaki Song*: the Wabanaki (also called the Abenaki or Abnaki) Indians
lived in what is now New Brunswick and Maine. They met Samuel de
Champlain in 1604 and later fought on the side of the French. These lines
are a translation of a Wabanaki poem.

Now I am left on this lonely island to die.
I wish the spirit of air would carry my breath to my love.   10
My love's canoe, like the sunlight, would shoot through
    the water to my side;
But I am left on this lonely island to die, with no one to
    pity me but the little birds.
My love is brave and strong; but, when he hears my fate,
    his stout heart will break;
And I am on this lonely island to die.
Now the night comes on, and all is silent but the owl.
    He sings a mournful song to his mate, in pity for me.   15
I will try to sleep. I wish the night spirit to hear my song;
    and he will tell my love of my fate; and when I awake,
    I shall see the one I love.
I am on this lonely island to die.

TRANS. CHARLES G. LELAND

## SHE'S LIKE THE SWALLOW

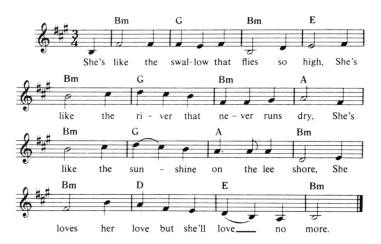

1. She's like the swallow that flies so high,
   She's like the river that never runs dry,
   She's like the sunshine on the lee shore,
   She loves her love but she'll love no more.

---

*lee* (l.3): sheltered side; away from the wind.

2. 'Twas down in the meadow this fair maid bent  5
   A-picking the primrose just as she went.
   The more she picked and the more she pulled,
   Until she gathered her apron full.

3. She climbed on yonder hill above
   To give a rose unto her love.  10
   She gave him one, she gave him three,
   She gave her heart for company.

4. And as they sat on yonder hill
   His heart grew hard, so harder still.
   He has two hearts instead of one.  15
   She says, 'Young man, what have you done?'

5. 'How foolish, foolish you must be
   To think I love no one but thee.
   The world's not made for one alone,
   I take delight in everyone.'  20

6. She took her roses and made a bed,
   A stony pillow for her head.
   She lay her down, no more did say,
   But let her roses fade away.

7. She's like the swallow that flies so high,  25
   She's like the river that never runs dry,
   She's like the sunshine on the lee shore,
   She loves her love but she'll love no more.

AUTHOR UNKNOWN


## THE LONELY LAND

Cedar and jagged fir
uplift sharp barbs
against the gray
and cloud-piled sky;
and in the bay  5
blown spume and windrift

---

*primrose* (l.6): name given to a large family of flowers, usually yellow; the word's origin is *prima rosa*—first rose.

*The Lonely Land, spume* (l.6): foam, froth.

and thin, bitter spray
snap
at the whirling sky;
and the pine trees                                    10
lean one way.

A wild duck calls
to her mate,
and the ragged
and passionate tones                                  15
stagger and fall,
and recover,
and stagger and fall,
on these stones—
are lost                                              20
in the lapping of water
on smooth, flat stones.

This is a beauty
of dissonance,
this resonance                                        25
of stony strand,
this smoky cry
curled over a black pine
like a broken
and wind-battered branch                              30
when the wind
bends the tops of the pines
and curdles the sky
from the north.

This is the beauty                                    35
of strength
broken by strength
and still strong.

A.J.M. SMITH (b. 1902)

---

*dissonance* (l.24): without harmony of parts; sounds that do not seem to fit
together.

# LOVE AND LONELINESS: QUESTIONS

## A. Love

### Sonnet 43: How Do I Love Thee (p. 24)

Elizabeth Barrett Browning wrote a series of 44 sonnets° which describe the development of her love for her husband Robert Browning (see p. 172). She intended that only he would read them, but after her death he had them published as he judged them to be finer than any sonnets written since Shakespeare's.

1. Examine the three sentences that make up lines 2-10. What is the main point of each sentence?
2. What are some connotations° or suggested meanings of the words "smiles" and "tears" in line 13?
3. How do the references to religious ideas and the comparisons in lines 7-9 contribute to the theme°?

### First Person Demonstrative (p. 24)

1. What problems has love caused for the speaker?
2. How does the expression of love in this poem compare to that in *How Do I Love Thee?* (p. 24)?
3. Do you think this poem is an effective statement about some aspects of love?

### The Passionate Shepherd to His Love (p. 25)

1. To what senses does the poem appeal? Give an example for each sense.
2. This poem was written about 400 years ago. Much of the language has been modernized, but the expressions are those of Marlowe's time. How does the language aid or hinder your understanding and appreciation of the poem?
3. If the poem were written today, what attractions might the young man offer his love?
4. Is this an effective love poem? Why or why not?
5. Compare this poem with the following one—Ogden Nash's *Love Under the Republicans (or Democrats)* (p. 26).

### Love Under the Republicans (or Democrats) (p. 26)

1. Compare this poem to Marlowe's *The Passionate Shepherd To His*

*Love* (p. 25). This parody° updates the original. Do you think it gives an accurate view of 20th century life?

2. How are the two poems different in tone°?
3. Do you find this poem humorous or gruesome? Find images° and ideas in the poem that help to create the mood° you find.

## Memory (p. 26)

1. Why are the descriptions of spring in stanza° one and night in stanza two especially effective? How do those descriptions add to the meaning of the poem?
2. What is the meaning of the line "We live within the light" in the last stanza?
3. Who might the speaker° of the poem be? In what situation might these words be spoken?
4. What does the title reveal about the theme? What is the theme of the poem?

## Marriage (p. 27)

1. What surprising conclusion about his marriage does the speaker reach?
2. Why do you think the poet used the image° of a thunderstorm to illustrate the thought of the poem?
3. What does that image add to the meaning of the poem?
4. What general statement about marriage does the poem make?

## Lost Jimmy Whelan (p. 28)

1. What power does love have according to this song?
2. We know the events described in the poem cannot be real, yet the poem still makes a statement about love. What is that statement?
3. Compare this ballad° with a modern love song of your own choice. Discuss the similarities and differences in the songs regarding:
   • their themes or statements about love;
   • their descriptions of love;
   • the language used to express the ideas;
   • other points you think are important.

# B. Loneliness

## Someone Who Used to Have Someone (p. 31)

1. Does the absence of normal punctuation and capitalization and the unusual line arrangement aid or hinder your understanding of the poem? Why?
2. What statement is made three times in the poem? What does that statement suggest about the theme?
3. Consider the feelings° the poem creates. Are they appropriate to the theme? How effective is the poem as a whole?

## Acquainted with the Night (p. 32)

1. What feelings are created by the poem?
2. What images or descriptions help to create those feelings?
3. What is meant by saying that the clock "Proclaimed the time was neither wrong nor right"?
4. How do the images or descriptions in this poem differ from those of Waddington's *Someone Who Used to Have Someone* (p. 31)? Which of the two poems do you think is more effective?

## The Forsaken (p. 33)

1. Parts I and II are similar in structure°. Compare the two parts under these headings:
   • the woman's actions;
   • the sequence of events;
   • the repetition of certain words, e.g. valiant, unshaken, rest (note how the meanings of the words change).
2. Compare the feelings expressed in the two parts of the poem. What words or phrases help to create these feelings?
3. What does this parallel structure add to the poem? Is it effective? Give reasons for your answer.
4. What examples of irony° are there in the poem?

## Wabanaki Song (p. 35)

1. What feelings does this poem arouse? What words and expressions stimulate those feelings?
2. Why is repetition of the line "I am left on this lonely island to die" especially effective?
3. Who might be the speaker of the poem? What might have happened to create this situation?
4. Divide the poem into stanzas using the line, "I am left on this lonely

island to die" as the first line of each stanza. Re-read the poem. Does this division change the effect or impact of the poem? If so, how?

5. What attitude to death is expressed in the poem?
6. Compare this poem with *The Forsaken* (p. 33).

## She's Like the Swallow (p. 36)

1. The first and last stanzas are the same and form an introduction and a conclusion. Why are the same words used for both purposes?
2. The girl is compared to a swallow, a river, and sunshine. Are these effective comparisons?
3. The meanings of these comparisons change between the first and last stanzas. What different meanings do they have?
4. What do these comparisons contribute to the feelings aroused by the poem?

## The Lonely Land (p. 37)

1. What "dissonance" or contrasts does the speaker find in the land?
2. In what way is the dissonance beautiful?
3. Explain the meaning of the last stanza which states the theme of the poem.
4. What is the general feeling of the poem? How does the poet create that feeling?

# 3 WAR AND HOPE

## Exploring Meaning: Tone and Intention

TONE° IS more easily noticed in speaking than it is in writing. For example, say the sentence, "You're my best friend" as follows:
- to show the person that you care deeply about him or her;
- sarcastically;
- to show how you feel about that person's doing something that has offended you.

Try the same sentence in other ways to show different emotions. Notice how your speech changes. Which words are emphasized in the different situations? Do you notice any difference in the speed at which the words are spoken? Are there differences in volume? How does the voice change at the end of the sentence each time?

In each case, the sense° of the words is the same, but the tone of voice reveals additional, or possibly even different, meanings. So it is with poetry. The poet subtly conveys an attitude to the reader through the tone of the poem. Any attitude that you can think of, whether it be friendly, admiring, loving, scarcastic, mocking, arrogant, prejudiced, etc., can be conveyed through a poem. The tone is more important in some poems than it is in others.

Up to now, we have been using the term "speaker". Perhaps you thought we should have used the word "poet" instead. But when we are reading a poem it is helpful to distinguish between the poet and the speaker° of the words. In this book we will refer to the speaker. In many poems, the poet creates a character to say the words. The poem can then be seen as a drama. There is a speaker (like an actor in a play); there may be one or more people who hear and perhaps also speak, or the reader may

be the intended hearer; there is a situation or setting in which the words are spoken.

Helpful questions to ask are:

• Who is speaking in the poem?
• To whom is he or she speaking?
• In what setting or situation are the words spoken?

At times the poet speaks directly to the reader, but assume first that the poet has created a character to say the words. Thinking about the speaker in this way will give you some insights into tone. Intention°, which is discussed on page 50 following, is often revealed by tone.

# War

War can be seen in many ways. In these poems, try to find not only the sense (the meaning of the words) and feeling (how the poet feels about the topic), but also the tone (the poet's attitude to the reader).

Poets and other people might consider questions such as these about war. What are you opinions?

• What is the purpose of war?
• Is anything useful achieved through war?
• Do the living have any responsibility to those who have died in battle?
• What is it like to fight?

### AGATHA CHRISTIE

being civil she saw poison
as a flaw in character
and the use of a knife
a case history in Freud

difficult to explain                                                        5
her dislike of jews

or why night upon night
she plotted solutions
to deaths she might have dreamed

her 200,000,000 readers                                                    10
how much longing for murder

---

*Agatha Christie*: British novelist who wrote a large number of popular murder mysteries.

the neatness of England
is and still remains

though in Belfast, say,
bombs have other reasons                                  15
and no one explains

ELI MANDEL (b. 1922)


## I HATE THAT DRUM'S DISCORDANT SOUND

I hate that drum's discordant sound,
Parading round, and round, and round:
To thoughtless youth it pleasure yields,
And lures from cities and from fields,
To sell their liberty for charms                          5
Of tawdry lace, and glittering arms;
And when Ambition's voice commands,
To march, and fight, and fall, in foreign lands.

I hate that drum's discordant sound,
Parading round, and round, and round:                     10
To me it talks of ravaged plains,
And burning towns, and ruined swains,
And mangled limbs, and dying groans,
The widows' tears, and orphans' moans;
And all that Misery's hand bestows,                       15
To fill the catalogue of human woes.

JOHN SCOTT (1730-1783)


## DREAMERS

Soldiers are citizens of death's gray land,
    Drawing no dividend from time's tomorrows.
In the great hour of destiny they stand,
    Each with his feuds, and jealousies, and sorrows.

---

*tawdry* (l.6): cheap and gaudy.
*swains* (l.12): youths.

---

*Dreamers, dividend* (l.2): a share of the profits of a company.

---

Soldiers are sworn to action; they must win 5
  Some flaming, fatal climax with their lives.
Soldiers are dreamers; when the guns begin
  They think of firelit homes, clean beds, and wives.

I see them in foul dug-outs, gnawed by rats,
  And in the ruined trenches, lashed with rain, 10
Dreaming of things they did with balls and bats,
  And mocked by hopeless longing to regain
Bank-holidays, and picture shows, and spats,
  And going to the office in the train.

SIEGFRIED SASSOON (1886-1967)


## ANTHEM FOR DOOMED YOUTH

What passing-bells for these who die as cattle?
Only the monstrous anger of the guns.
Only the stuttering rifles' rapid rattle
Can patter out their hasty orisons.
No mockeries for them; no prayers nor bells, 5
Nor any voice of mourning save the choirs,—
The shrill, demented choirs of wailing shells;
And bugles calling for them from sad shires.

What candles may be held to speed them all?
Not in the hands of boys, but in their eyes 10
Shall shine the holy glimmers of good-byes.
The pallor of girls' brows shall be their pall;
Their flowers the tenderness of patient minds,
And each slow dusk a drawing-down of blinds.

WILFRED OWEN (1893-1918)


*spats* (l.13): a covering formerly worn over the shoe and ankle; spats were
  worn by well-dressed business men of the early 20th century.

*Anthem for Doomed Youth, passing-bells* (l.1): bells rung at the time of a
  person's death; funeral bells.
*orisons* (l.4): prayers.
*pallor* (l.12): paleness.
*pall* (l.12): cloth spread over a coffin.

## IN FLANDERS FIELDS

In Flanders fields the poppies blow
Between the crosses, row on row,
    That mark our place; and in the sky
    The larks, still bravely singing, fly
Scarce heard amid the guns below.             5

We are the Dead. Short days ago
We lived, felt dawn, saw sunset glow,
    Loved and were loved, and now we lie,
    In Flanders fields.

Take up our quarrel with the foe:            10
To you from failing hands we throw
    The torch; be yours to hold it high.
    If ye break faith with us who die
We shall not sleep, though poppies grow
    In Flanders fields               15

JOHN McCRAE (1872-1918)


## WHAT DO I REMEMBER OF THE EVACUATION

What do I remember of the evacuation?
I remember my father telling Tim and me
About the mountains and the train
And the excitement of going on a trip.
What do I remember of the evacuation?      5
I remember my mother wrapping
A blanket around me and my
Pretending to fall asleep so she would be happy
Though I was so excited I couldn't sleep
(I hear there were people herded         10
Into the Hastings Park like cattle.

---

*In Flanders Fields*: a large cemetery for the war dead in Belgium.
*poppies* (l.1): bright red flowers planted in memory of those who died in
  battle (and from which opium is made).

---

*What Do I Remember of the Evacuation* (l.1): during the Second World
  War (1939-1945) thousands of Japanese who were Canadian citizens or
  landed immigrants were forcibly moved from their homes in southern
  British Columbia to special camps farther inland. The authorities feared
  that some of them might have been Japanese spies.

---

Families were made to move in two hours
Abandoning everything, leaving pets
And possessions at gun point.
I hear families were broken up                                    15
Men were forced to work. I heard
It whispered late at night
That there was suffering) and
I missed my dolls.
What do I remember of the evacuation?                            20
I remember Miss Foster and Miss Tucker
Who still live in Vancouver
And who did what they could
And loved the children and who gave me
A puzzle to play with on the train.                              25
And I remember the mountains and I was
Six years old and I swear I saw a giant
Gulliver of Gulliver's Travels scanning the horizon
And when I told my mother she believed it too
And I remember how careful my parents were                       30
Not to bruise us with bitterness
And I remember the puzzle of Lorraine Life
Who said "Don't insult me" when I
Proudly wrote my name in Japanese
And Tim flew the Union Jack                                      35
When the war was over but Lorraine
And her friends spat on us anyway
And I prayed to God who loves
All the children in his sight
That I might be white.                                           40

JOY KOGAWA (b. 1935)


## I HAVE A RENDEZVOUS WITH DEATH

I have a rendezvous with Death
At some disputed barricade,
When Spring comes back with rustling shade
And apple-blossoms fill the air—
I have a rendezvous with Death                                   5
When Spring brings back blue days and fair.

It may be he shall take my hand

---

*rendezvous* (l.1): appointment.

And lead me into his dark land
And close my eyes and quench my breath—
It may be I shall pass him still.                                    10
I have a rendezvous with Death
On some scarred slope of battered hill,
When Spring comes round again this year
And the first meadow-flowers appear.

God knows 'twere better to be deep                          15
Pillowed in silk and scented down,
Where Love throbs out in blissful sleep,
Pulse nigh to pulse, and breath to breath,
Where hushed awakenings are dear . . .
But I've a rendezvous with Death                             20
At midnight in some flaming town.
When spring trips north again this year,
And I to my pledged word am true,
I shall not fail that rendezvous.

ALAN SEEGER (1889-1916)

INTENTION⁰ IS the poet's purpose in composing the poem. The intention
can be found by asking yourself, "Why does the speaker of the poem say
what he or she says?"

The various kinds of meaning, such as sense (p. 23), feeling (p. 31), tone
(p. 43) and now intention, are not confined to poems. They are present in
all forms of communication. For example, how often have you heard or
said questions and statements like these:

- "Would you mind repeating that?" (sense)
- "You don't seem very eager to do it." (feeling)
- "It's not what you said, it's how you said it." (tone)
- "Now why did you say that?" (intention)

To enjoy a poem, we must understand it. To understand it, we must
look for its kinds of meaning.

# Hope

When we are depressed because things go badly for us, we look for some way out of our unhappiness. We look for hope. Poets have offered hopeful statements on various topics:
- Where does hope come from?
- Is there anything that we can be sure of that will give us hope?
- What symbols or people can be models of hope for us?
- Is any situation totally hopeless?

## THERE WILL COME SOFT RAINS
*(War Time)*

There will come soft rains and the smell of the ground,
And swallows circling with their shimmering sound;

And frogs in the pools singing at night,
And wild plum-trees in tremulous white.

Robins will wear their feathery fire         5
Whistling their whims on a low fence-wire;

And not one will know of the war, not one
Will care at last when it is done.

Not one would mind, neither bird nor tree,
If mankind perished utterly;         10

And Spring herself, when she woke at dawn,
Would scarcely know that we were gone.

SARA TEASDALE (1884-1933)

## ULYSSES
*—an excerpt*

The lights begin to twinkle from the rocks;
The long day wanes; the slow moon climbs; the deep
Moans round with many voices. Come, my friends.

---

*Ulysses*: the Latin name for Odysseus, the Greek hero of *The Iliad* and *The Odyssey*. Although old and weakened, Odysseus slew fifty suitors who, thinking that he was dead, were demanding that his wife Penelope marry one of them.
*wanes* (l.2): draws to a close; declines in power.

'Tis not too late to seek a newer world.
Push off, and sitting well in order smite      5
The sounding furrows; for my purpose holds
To sail beyond the sunset, and the baths
Of all the western stars, until I die.
It may be that the gulfs will wash us down;
It may be we shall touch the Happy Isles,      10
And see the great Achilles, whom we knew.
Though much is taken, much abides; and though
We are not now that strength which in old days
Moved earth and heaven, that which we are, we are—
One equal temper of heroic hearts,      15
Made weak by time and fate, but strong in will
To strive, to seek, to find, and not to yield.

ALFRED LORD TENNYSON (1809-1892)


## SONNET 29

When, in disgrace with Fortune and men's eyes,
I all alone beweep my outcast state,
And trouble deaf heaven with my bootless cries,
And look upon myself and curse my fate,
Wishing me like to one more rich in hope,      5
Featured like him, like him with friends possessed,
Desiring this man's art, and that man's scope,
With what I most enjoy contented least;
Yet in these thoughts myself almost despising,
Haply I think on thee, and then my state,      10

---

*smite* (l.5): strike.
*furrows* (l.6): troughs between the waves.
*baths* (l.7): in this sense, the sky surrounding the stars.
*Happy Isles* (l.10): where just people go after death.
*Achilles* (l.11): famous Greek hero, slain by an arrow in the heel during the
 battle of Troy. His weapons were given to Ulysses.
*temper* (l.15): state of mind; also the sense of being prepared or
 strengthened, as in tempering steel.

---

*Sonnet 29, disgrace* (l.1): disfavor.
*outcast* (l.2): rejected, despised.
*bootless* (l.3): useless; pointless.
*featured* (l.6): look like him, i.e. to be handsome.
*scope* (l.7): knowledge; learning.

Like to the lark at break of day arising
From sullen earth, sings hymns at heaven's gate;
 For thy sweet love remembered such wealth brings
 That then I scorn to change my state with kings.

WILLIAM SHAKESPEARE (1564-1616)


## PSALM 23: THE LORD IS MY SHEPHERD

1 The Lord is my shepherd; I shall not want.
2 He maketh me to lie down in green pastures: he leadeth
 me beside the still waters.
3 He restoreth my soul: he leadeth me in the paths of
 righteousness for his name's sake.
4 Yea, though I walk though the valley of the shadow of
 death, I will fear no evil: for thou art with me; thy rod
 and thy staff they comfort me.
5 Thou preparest a table before me in the presence of mine
 enemies: thou anointest my head with oil; my cup
 runneth over.
6 Surely goodness and mercy shall follow me all the days
 of my life: and I will dwell in the house of the Lord   for
ever.


## SONG

The great sea
Has set me adrift,
It moves me as the weed in a great river,
Earth and the great weather
Move me,           5
Have carried me away
And move my inward parts with joy.

AUTHOR UNKNOWN

---

*Psalm*: a sacred song or poem.
*anointest* (l.5): blesses with holy oil.

## OUTWITTED

He drew a circle that shut me out—
Heretic, rebel, a thing to flout.
But Love and I had the wit to win:
We drew a circle that took him in!

EDWIN MARKAM (1852-1940)

## LOCKSLEY HALL
*—an excerpt*

For I dipped into the future, far as human eye could see,
Saw the Vision of the world, and all the wonder that would
be;

Saw the heavens fill with commerce, argosies of magic sails,
Pilots of the purple twilight, dropping down with costly
bales;

Heard the heavens fill with shouting, and there rained a
ghastly dew                                                    5
From the nations' airy navies grappling in the central blue;

Far along the world-wide whisper of the south wind rushing
warm,
With the standards of the peoples plunging through the
thunder-storm;

Till the war drum throbbed no longer, and the battle-flags
were furled
In the Parliament of man, the Federation of the world.    10

---

*heretic* (1.2): one who holds unorthodox beliefs—that is, beliefs (particularly religious beliefs) which are not generally accepted.

---

*Locksley Hall, argosies* (1.3): fleets of ships; from the Greek ship "Argo" in which Jason led Hercules, Orpheus and other Greek heroes in search of the golden fleece.
*standards* (1.8): a flag, sculptured figure or other object raised on a pole which serves as a nation's or ruler's symbol. It is carried into battle to indicate the rallying point of an army.

There the common sense of most shall hold a fretful realm
   in awe,
And the kindly earth shall slumber, lapped in universal law.

ALFRED LORD TENNYSON (1809-1892)


## RÉSUMÉ

Razors pain you;
Rivers are damp;
Acids stain you;
And drugs cause cramp.
Guns aren't lawful;
Nooses give;
Gas smells awful;
You might as well live.

DOROTHY PARKER (1893-1967)


# WAR AND HOPE: QUESTIONS

# A. War

**Agatha Christie (p. 45)**

1. The speaker does not attack Agatha Christie personally, but uses her as a symbol°. What or whom does she symbolize?
2. What irony° or contrast in our lives does the speaker draw to our attention?
3. The usual sentence punctuation has been omitted in this poem. Decide where the sentences would begin and end. What other common items have been omitted?
4. Who might the speaker be? To whom might he or she be speaking? What might the situation be?
5. What tone is conveyed by the poem? What words or expressions help to create that tone?

**I Hate That Drum's Discordant Sound (p. 46)**

1. What contrasting pictures are presented in the two stanzas°?
2. Why are the first two lines of each stanza the same?

3. What is the tone of the poem? What words and phrases help to create that tone?

## Dreamers (p. 46)

1. Note that three views of soldiers are presented in the first stanza, each beginning with the words, "Soldiers are." How do these three pictures contrast with the descriptions in the last stanza?
2. What is the theme of the poem?
3. What view of war is presented? How does that view differ from the views presented in the other poems in this group? Are any of the other poems similar to this one? In what ways?
4. What is the tone of the poem? How is that tone created?

## Anthem for Doomed Youth (p. 47)

1. List the words and phrases in the poem that relate to religion and churches. How are these terms related to the theme° of the poem?
2. What feelings° does the poem create? What words and expressions help to create those feelings?
3. Many of the descriptions in this poem are effective not because of contrast, but because of startling similarities. What unusual comparisons does the poet make? How does the poem's question and answer format contribute to its effect?
4. Do the theme, the feelings and the tone of this poem reinforce each other? Is this an effective poem?

## In Flanders Fields (p. 48)

1. What contrasts are presented in the poem? What effect do they have?
2. As in the *Anthem for Doomed Youth*, there is much repetition. What is the purpose of the repetition in this poem?
3. Who are speaking in the poem? What challenge do they present?
4. What is the tone of the poem? How is that tone created?
5. How is the theme of this poem different from the themes of the previous poems about war?

## What Do I Remember of the Evacuation (p. 48)

1. The poem presents a form of irony° in the contrast between the child's point of view and the horrors that were occurring. How does this irony contribute to the overall effect of the poem?
2. How does the speaker show that the experience had a lasting effect on the child?
3. Briefly summarize what the speaker remembers of the evacuation.

4. What is the tone of the poem? What is the theme? Is tone important to this poem?

## I Have a Rendezvous with Death (p. 49)

1. What contrasts are presented in the poem?
2. What lines and phrases are repeated? Why are they repeated?
3. What pictures run through the speaker's mind as he thinks about death?
4. Is the poem optimistic or pessimistic? Give reasons for your answer.

# B. Hope

## There Will Come Soft Rains (p. 51)

1. Why did the poet choose the images of rain, swallows and robins to illustrate her ideas?
2. What is the speaker's opinion of the place of humans in the universe? What are the tone and intention of the poem? Support your opinions by references to the poem.
3. Why is the conclusion of the poem startling?
4. What perspective on war does the poem give?

## Ulysses (p. 51)

1. What two impressions of the warriors are given in the poem?
2. What lines summarize the main thought?
3. Why did the poet choose a character like Ulysses to express his thoughts?
4. What might have been the poet's intention in writing this poem?

## Sonnet 29 (p. 53)

1. What is the theme of the poem? What does the theme suggest about the intention of the poem?
2. What two main moods° or feelings are presented in the poem? Quote words and lines which support your opinion.
3. How do these feelings relate to the theme?
4. What raises the speaker of the poem out of his loneliness and despair?
5. If this poem were divided into two, where would you make the division? Give reasons for your choice.

**Psalm 23 (p. 54)**

1. What image° of the Lord is presented in verses 1-4? What image of the Lord is presented in the last two verses?
2. What is the connection between these two images? Why did the psalmist (the writer of the psalm) chose them?
3. What view of human life does the psalm present? For what purpose might it have been written?
4. If this psalm were written today, what images might a poet choose?

**Song (p. 54)**

1. Although alone, the speaker feels joy. Why?
2. From what does the speaker seem to draw strength and faith?
3. Compare and contrast this poem with *There Will Come Soft Rains* (p. 00). Consider the sense, feeling, tone and intention of both poems.

**Outwitted (p. 55)**

1. What is the intention of this poem?
2. How are the sense, feeling, tone and intention interrelated in the poem?

**Locksley Hall (p. 55)**

1. This poem was written in 1842. What prophecies in it have come true?
2. Which of its prophecies have not been fulfilled?
3. What is the dominant tone of the poem? What gives it that tone?
4. What might be the intent of the poem?

**Résumé (p. 56)**

1. What is the tone of this poem? What is its intent?
2. Does the poem make its point effectively? Give reasons for your opinion.
3. Résumé has come to mean, in its common English usage, a list outlining the qualifications an individual has and the things he or she has achieved. In French it means "to begin again." Do both meanings apply here? How?

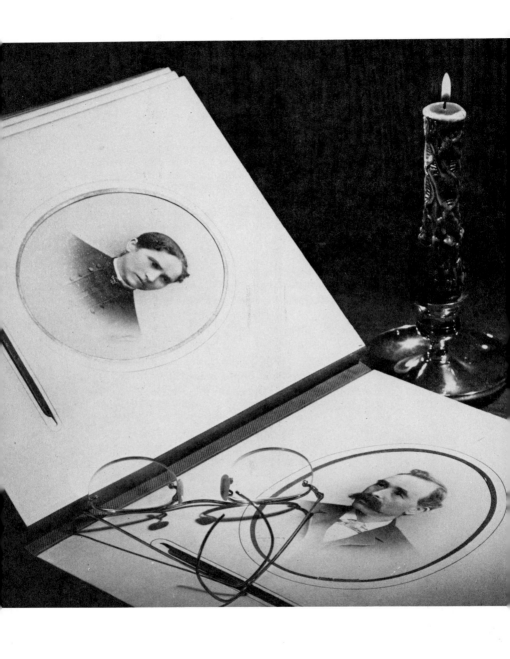

# 4 PEOPLE AND PLACES

## Exploring Meaning: Structure and Thought

A poem is an organized expression of the poet's experience. At first you may find some poems hard to understand because you have not had an experience like the one discussed in the poem. Understanding the poet's expression of his or her experience requires us to reverse the poet's activity in writing it. The poet has an experience which stimulates thoughts which are shaped into words. The reader interprets the words to understand the thoughts to share in the experience. This relationship can be represented schematically:

The poet ⁻ *Experience* ⌇ *Thoughts* ⌇ *Words* ⌐ The reader

So the reader must start with the words, and the words may be the only thing that reader and poet have in common.

THE POEM'S STRUCTURE° consists of words grouped in some meaningful way. To start with, words are grouped into clauses and sentences. You have already seen how important it is to note the sentences a poem contains. In prose the sentences are grouped into paragraphs. In a poem the words are grouped into stanzas°. Think of a stanza as if it were a paragraph in an essay or a story.

You know that paragraphs have unity and coherence and that they are the building blocks of an essay or story. Each paragraph is a step in the development of the total thought of the composition. Think of stanzas in a poem in the same way. Each is a step in the development of the thought of the poem.

With some poems, a sentence may run across stanza boundaries. Do not let this bother you. Remember that the language of poetry is tightly packed with meaning. The poet may deliberately break a sentence into stanzas to force the reader to consider each part of the sentence thoroughly.

In these poems about people, look for the overall structure of each poem. Note the sentence structures and punctuation, and also think about the statement each stanza makes. If the poem contains only one stanza, think about why the poet did not break it into more parts. An awareness of a poem's structure can give important clues to the poet's thinking (discussed on page 72 following).

# People

We have all had experiences with people. People amuse us, interest us, make us laugh, make us angry. We admire some people and dislike others. And of course each of us is a person.

- What kind of person are you?
- How important is your relationship to other people?
- What is your place in the large groups of people that make up your community, your country, your world?
- What kinds of people do you enjoy meeting? Why?

### ROSE'S MOTHER WAS NOT GOOD AT KEEPING HOUSE

If Rose's mother
hated a house
it would burn down.

Oh, not on purpose,
no insurance man                                          5
issuing the cheque
ever questioned the cause.

It was only
that if one day
the rooms seemed small,                                   10
the closets set
too close together
in the wall,
or the staircase began
to offend somehow,                                        15
it would soon
be all reduced to ash,

not suspiciously,
only inevitably.

One Hallowe'en                                                   20
Rose's mother
left alone
to keep the home fires burning
decided
her present house                                               25
was not a pleasant house
to be left alone in,
so she made a goblin face
on a sheet
and put it over the lamp                                        30
by the window
for the kids to see
and went out.

Next day
they found                                                      35
all the piano keys
melted into each other
like one big note.

Rose had lived
in a lot of houses.                                             40
"After the fifth
or sixth,"
she says
"When mother said
she didn't like a house,                                        45
father listened."

ROSEMARY AUBERT (b. 1946)


## BEFORE TWO PORTRAITS OF MY MOTHER

I love the beautiful young girl of this
portrait, my mother, painted years ago
when her forehead was white, and there was no
shadow in the dazzling Venetian glass

of her gaze. But this other likeness shows            5
the deep trenches across her forehead's white

---

*Venetian glass* (1.4): a fine, very delicate kind of glassware.

marble. The rose poem of her youth that
her marriage sang is far behind. Here is

my sadness: I compare these portraits, one
of a joy-radiant brow, the other care-                          10
heavy: sunrise—and the thick coming on

of night. And yet how strange my ways appear,
for when I look at these faded lips my heart
smiles, but at the smiling girl my tears start.

EMILE NELLIGAN (1879-1941)


## FATHER

Twice he took me in his hands and shook
me like a sheaf of wheat, the way a dog shakes
a snake, as if he meant to knock out my tongue
and grind it under his heel right there
on the kitchen floor. I never remembered            5
what he said or the warnings he gave; she
always told me afterwards, when he
had left and I had stopped my crying. I
was eleven that year and for seven more years
I watched his friends laughing and him            10
with his great hands rising and falling
with every laugh, smashing down on his knees
and making the noise of a tree when it cracks
in winter. Together they drank chokecherry
wine and talked of dead friends and the            15
old times when they were young, and because
I never thought of getting old, their
youth was the first I knew of dying.

Sunday before church he would trim
his fingernails with the hunting knife            20
his East German cousins had sent, the same
knife he used for castrating pigs and
skinning deer: things that had nothing
to do with Sunday. Communion once
a month, a shave every third day, a            25
good chew of snuff, these were the things
that helped a man to stand in the sun for
eight hours a day, to sweat through each
cold hail storm without a word, to freeze
fingers and feet to cut winter wood, to do            30

the work that bent his back a little more
each day toward the ground.

Last Christmas, for the first time, he
gave presents, unwrapped and bought
with pension money. He drinks mostly coffee          35
now, sleeping late and shaving everyday.
Even the hands have changed: white, soft,
unused hands. Still he seems content
to be this old, to be sleeping in the middle
of the afternoon with his mouth open as if there     40
is no further need for secrets, as if he is
no longer afraid to call his children fools
for finding different answers, different lives.

DALE ZIEROTH (b. 1946)


## GRANDFATHER

Grandfather
          Jabez Harry Bowering
strode across the Canadian prairie
hacking down trees
                    & building churches                5
delivering personal baptist sermons in them
leading Holy holy holy lord god almighty songs in them
red haired man squared off in the pulpit
reading Saul on the road to Damascus at them

Left home                                              10
          big walled Bristol town
at age eight
          to make a living
buried his stubby fingers in root snarled earth
for a suit of clothes & seven hundred gruelly meals a year  15

---

*Holy, holy, holy lord god almighty* (1.7): the first line of a popular hymn.
*Saul on the road to Damascus* (1.9): Saul, who was bitterly opposed to
  Christianity, was converted when God spoke to him in a flash of light
  which appeared to him as he travelled to Damascus. He then took the
  name Paul, and his epistles (letters) to various early Christian
  communities are a key element of the Christian tradition.
*Bristol* (1.11): a city in England.

taking an anabaptist cane across the back every day
for four years till he was whipt out of England

Twelve years old
         & across the ocean alone
to apocalyptic Canada                                 20
                 Ontario of bone bending labor
six years on the road to Damascus till his eyes were blinded
with the blast of Christ & he wandered west
to Brandon among wheat kings & heathen Saturday nights
young red haired Bristol boy shoveling coal          25
in the basement of Brandon college five in the morning

Then built his first wooden church & married
a sick girl who bore two live children & died
leaving several pitiful letters & the Manitoba night

He moved west with another wife & built children &
       churches                                    30
Saskatchewan Alberta British Columbia Holy holy holy
lord god almighty
                 struck his labored bones with pain
& left him a postmaster prodding grandchildren with crutches
another dead wife & a glass bowl of photographs      35
& holy books unopened save the bible by the bed

Till he died the day before his eighty fifth birthday
in a Catholic hospital of sheets white as his hair

GEORGE BOWERING (b. 1938)


## JIM LOVENZANNA

i remember sitting in jimmy hoy's place one sunday
listening to old lovenzanna and others recalling stories
about the thirties
lovenzanna spoke of the time before he moved to the
       village
how he and a neighbour planted crops four years straight   5
though nothing grew (the land slowly drifting away)

---

*Anabaptist* (l.16): a strict Protestant sect opposed to infant baptism and
    requiring adult baptism.
*apocalyptic* (l.20): pertaining to a revelation, especially one about the end of
    the world.

how the neighbour grew sad and spoke less each time they
   met
and finally lost faith in faith
no longer speaking at all in the end—
lovenzanna remembered something as though it were a
   dream:                                                                    10
*i was driving past his place one day*
*it was cloudless and bright and very hot that day*
*and i saw the threshing machine going full blast*
*and nick sweating beside it with a huge rack load of*
   *thistles*
*i felt kind of funny and thought maybe i was seeing things* 15
*anyway i stopped my team and walked over to him and*
   *said*
*"nick—what the hell's up?"*
*nick's eyes looked like twin moons as he grinned and*
   *answered*
*"threshing jim—must be going 40 bushels to an acre*
*the best crop i've had in years"*                              20
lovenzanna said the mounties arrived the next day
and took nick away to weyburn—
he returned a few months later and the following year
the mounties found him driving his binder
through a dust storm (once again harvesting thistles)         25
when they approached him
he pulled a monkey wrench from the tool box
and began waving it at them—in the other hand he waved
a crumpled sheet of paper and shouted their way:
*look godammit*                                                 30
*i'm not crazy and i have proof i've bin to weyburn*
*now what the hell do you bastards have to prove you're*
   *not nuts?*

another spring years later
lovenzanna said to friends drinking coffee in hoy's place:
*before i die i want to harvest the biggest crop*              35
*that's ever been seen in the south country*

that summer
summerfallowing on a new quarter added to his prairie
   empire
lovenzanna moved to another field
it was a hot july day as he made the first round           40
slowly falling asleep at the wheel he drove
into an abandoned root cellar in the farmyard on the field's
   edge

(late that night men from the village found him pinned
under the tractor
with a crumbled doorframe across his chest)                    45

in the autumn a dozen men got together to combine the
        wheat
for the widow
they built a floor in the old barn for the last 5,000
of 33,000 bushels harvested

the evening mrs lovenzanna served the last supper          50
one farmer said:
*too bad old jim ain't here to see it all in the granaries*
mrs lovenzanna nodded and
a bottle of whiskey no one had noticed before
was being held next to her heart                                      55
she smiled and placed the bottle on the table—and said:
*a little of something jim would have given the kids*
*this christmas*

as a farmer finished pouring a glass for each man
they raised their glasses and said:                                   60
*well—here's to old jim*

ANDREW SUKNASKI (b. 1942)


## ANNABEL LEE

It was many and many a year ago,
        In a kingdom by the sea
That a maiden there lived whom you may know
        By the name of ANNABEL LEE;
And this maiden she lived with no other thought          5
        Than to love and be loved by me.

I was a child and *she* was a child,
        In this kingdom by the sea,
But we loved with a love that was more than love—
        I and my ANNABEL LEE—                                    10
With a love that the wingèd seraphs of heaven
        Coveted her and me.

And this was the reason that, long ago,
        In this kingdom by the sea,

---

*seraphs* (l.11): a class of angels noted for the strength of their love.
*coveted* (l.12): desired, longed for.

A wind blew out of a cloud, chilling                    15
    My beautiful ANNABEL LEE;
So that her high-born kinsmen came
    And bore her away from me,
To shut her up in a sepulchre
    In this kingdom by the sea.                          20

The angels, not half so happy in heaven,
    Went envying her and me—
Yes!—that was the reason (as all men know,
    In this kingdom by the sea)
That the wind came out of the cloud by night,           25
    Chilling and killing my ANNABEL LEE.

But our love it was stronger by far than the love
    Of those who were older than we—
    Of many far wiser than we—
And neither the angels in heaven above,                 30
    Nor the demons down under the sea,
Can ever dissever my soul from the soul
    Of the beautiful ANNABEL LEE:

For the moon never beams, without bringing me dreams
    Of the beautiful ANNABEL LEE,                        35
And the stars never rise, but I feel the bright eyes
    Of the beautiful ANNABEL LEE:
And so, all the night-tide, I lie down by the side
Of my darling—my darling—my life and my bride,
    In the sepulchre there by the sea—                   40
    In her tomb by the sounding sea.

EDGAR ALLAN POE (1809-1849)


## THE CANNIBAL FLEA

It was many and many a year ago
In a District called E. C.,
That a Monster dwelt whom I came to know
By the name of Cannibal Flea,
And the brute was possessed with no other thought        5
Than to live—and to live on me!

---

*sepulchre* (l.19): tomb; burial place.
*dissever* (l.32): separate, divide.

I was in bed, and he was in bed
In the District named E. C.,
When first in his thirst so accurst he burst
Upon me, the Cannibal Flea,                                    10
With a bite that felt as if some one had driven
A bayonet into me.

And this was the reason why long ago
In that District named E. C.
I tumbled out of my bed, willing                              15
To capture the Cannibal Flea,
Who all the night until morning came
Kept boring into me!
It wore me down to a skeleton
In the District hight E. C.                                   20

From that hour I sought my bed—eleven—
Till daylight he tortured me.
Yes!—that was the reason (as all men know
In that District named E. C.)
I so often jumped out of my bed by night                     25
Willing the killing of Cannibal Flea.

But his hops they were longer by far than the hops
Of creatures much larger than he—
Of parties more long-legged than he;
And neither the powder nor turpentine drops,                 30
Nor the persons engaged by me,
Were so clever as ever to stop me the hop
Of the terrible Cannibal Flea.

For at night with a scream, I am waked from my dream
By the terrible Cannibal Flea;                                35
And at morn I ne'er rise without bites—of such size—
From the terrible Cannibal Flea.

TOM HOOD JR. (1835-1874)

---

*hight* (l.20): a very old word meaning "called" or "named" now used only in
poems.

---

## CANADIANS

Here are
our signatures:
geese, fish, eskimo
faces, girl-guide
cookies, ink-drawings                                          5
tree-plantings, summer
storms and winter
emanations.

We look
like a geography but                                          10
just scratch us
and we bleed
history, are full
of modest misery
are sensitive                                                15
to double-talk double-take
(and double-cross)
in a country
too wide
to be single in.                                             20

Are we real or
did someone invent
us, was it Henry
Hudson Etienne Brûlé
or a carnival                                                25
of village girls?
Was it
a flock of nuns
a pity of indians
a gravyboat of                                               30
fur-traders, professional
explorers or those
amateur map-makers
our Fathers
of Confederation?                                            35

Wherever you are
Charles Tupper Alexander

---

*emanations* (l.8): things which come forth from some source. For example,
light emanates from the sun; a spring of water emanates from the earth.

Galt Darcy McGee George
Cartier Ambrose Shea
Henry Crout Father                                    40
Ragueneau Lord Selkirk
and John A.—however
far into northness
you have walked—
when we call you                                      45
turn around and
don't look so surprised.

MIRIAM WADDINGTON (b. 1917)

THE POET'S THOUGHT IS the key to broadening our own experience.
Because the experiences expressed in the poem may be strange to us, we
must, as Samuel Taylor Coleridge said, make a "willing suspension of
disbelief." That is, for a time we must accept what the writer says as true.
By acquainting ourselves with different points of view, we understand
people's varying reactions to their experiences. For example, if we are sure
that war is horrible and then reject all poems that say war is glorious, we
cut ourselves off from a broader experience. We need not agree with some
poets, but we should at least try to see what they are saying before we
reject their statements.

Through poems we can find how people thought about their experiences in other times and in other places. We can see the points of view and
opinions of other people and thereby understand our own experiences
more deeply. But to achieve these goals, we must set aside our own
thoughts and opinions and try to find the poet's.

When reading a poem as a communication, you start with the poet's
words and find out something about the poet's thoughts and experiences.
Another way to think about a poem is to see it as a dramatic situation in
which one participant (actor) speaks to one or more others, who may be
present in the poem or who may be outside of it. You, the reader, may be
the poet's audience.

Finding the poet's thought will also help you to find his or her feeling°,
tone° and intention°. Ask yourself these questions:

• Who is speaking?
• To whom is he or she speaking?
• In what situation or setting are both speaker and audience?

You will notice that these questions require you to use your imagination,
to let the words of the poem set off a series of pictures and thoughts in

your mind. By asking yourself these questions, you can re-create the dramatic situation of the poem. That in turn will allow you to reach more deeply into the poet's way of seeing the topic°.

# Places

We have all visited places that have deeply affected us: Some places we remember with affection, others with sadness or displeasure. At times, a place can symbolize something much broader in scope. For example, a snow-capped peak can symbolize the Rocky Mountains, or it could symbolize loneliness or a person's striving for something.

As you read these poems, consider these questions:
• Is the poet merely describing the place?
• Does the place have meaning beyond its reality for the poet?
• How does the poet feel about the place?
• What seems to be the poet's intention in writing about the place?

Before starting to read the poems, you might also think about and discuss your most loved and most hated places. Why do you have the feelings towards them that you have? What do the places mean to you?


## IN THE FOREST

In the forest
 down the cut roads
  the sides of them
gravel rolls
  thundering down,      5
  each small stone
a rock waterfall
  that frightens me
  sitting in my ditch.

I smoke my last         10
 cigarette rolled
  with bible paper,
listen to the stone
  cascading down,
   some of it bouncing    15
off my hunched shoulders.
  Above me the dark grass
   hangs over the edge
like a badly-fitted wig

10 feet above me.      20
I dream of the animals
    that may sulk there,
        deer snake and bear
dangerous and inviolable.
    as I am not inviolable.      25
    Even the gentle deer
scare me at midnight,
    no-one else for 100 miles,
      even the sucking snakes
small and lithe as syrup.      30
    The forest is not silent,
water smashes its way,
    rocks bounce, wind magnifies
its usual noise
    and my shivering fear      35
    makes something alive
move in the trees,
    shift in the grass
    10 feet above me.

I am too frightened      40
    to move or to stay,
      sweating in the wind.
An hour later
    I convulse unthinking
and run, run, run down the cold road,      45

JOHN NEWLOVE (b. 1938)


## MORNING ON THE LIÈVRE

Far above us where a jay
Screams his matins to the day,
Capped with gold and amethyst,
Like a vapour from the forge
Of a giant somewhere hid,      5

---

*inviolable* (1.24): unable to be injured or violated; sacred.

---

*Morning on the Lièvre*: a tributary of the Ottawa River, flowing into it from
   the north-east (Quebec).
*matins* (1.2): a morning song; also a morning prayer.
*amethyst* (1.3): precious stone of clear purple or bluish violet.

Out of hearing of the clang
Of his hammer, skirts of mist
Slowly up the woody gorge
Lift and hang.

Softly as a cloud we go,                                    10
Sky above and sky below,
Down the river; and the dip
Of the paddles scarcely breaks,
With the little silvery drip
Of the water as it shakes                                   15
From the blades, the crystal deep
Of the silence of the morn,
Of the forest yet asleep;
And the river reaches borne
In a mirror, purple gray,                                   20
Sheer away
To the misty line of light,
Where the forest and the stream
In the shadow meet and plight,
Like a dream.                                              25

From amid a stretch of reeds,
Where the lazy river sucks
All the water as it bleeds
From a little curling creek,
And the muskrats peer and sneak                             30
In around the sunken wrecks
Of a tree that swept the skies
Long ago,
On a sudden seven ducks
With a splashy rustle rise,                                 35
Stretching out their seven necks,
One before, and two behind,
And the others all arow,
And as steady as the wind
With a swivelling whistle go,
Through the purple shadow led,                              40
Till we only hear their whir
In behind a rocky spur,
Just ahead.

ARCHIBALD LAMPMAN (1861-1899)

---

*plight* (l.24): to promise oneself to another, usually in the sense of becoming
  engaged.

## THE WINTER LAKES

Out in a world of death, far to the northward lying,
  Under the sun and the moon, under the dusk and the day;
Under the glimmer of stars and the purple of sunsets dying,
  Wan and waste and white, stretch the great lakes away.

Never a bud of spring, never a laugh of summer,                    5
  Never a dream of love, never a song of bird;
But only the silence and white, the shores that grow chiller and
    dumber,
  Wherever the ice-winds sob, and the griefs of winter are heard.

Crags that are black and wet out of the gray lake looming,
  Under the sunset's flush, and the pallid, faint glimmer of dawn;   10
Shadowy, ghost-like shores, where midnight surfs are booming
  Thunders of wintry woe over the spaces wan.

Lands that loom like spectres, whited regions of winter,
  Wastes of desolate woods, deserts of water and shore;
A world of winter and death, within these regions who enter,       15
  Lost to summer and life, go to return no more.

Moons that glimmer above, waters that lie white under,
  Miles and miles of lake far out under the night;
Foaming crests of waves, surfs that shoreward thunder,
  Shadowy shapes that flee, haunting the spaces white.              20

Lonely hidden bays, moon-lit, ice-rimmed, winding,
  Fringed by forests and crags, haunted by shadowy shores;
Hushed from the outward strife, where the mighty surf is grinding
  Death and hate on the rocks, as sandward and landward it roars.

WILLIAM WILFRED CAMPBELL (1861-1919)


## MY GARDEN

A little blade of grass I see,
Its banner waving white and free,
And I wonder if in time to come
'Twill be a great big onion;
We cannot tell, we do not know,                                     5
For oft we reap and didn't sow;
We plant the hairy coconut,

---

*wan* (l.4): pale; sickly.

With hope serene and sturdy—but
We cannot tell, for who can say,
We plant the oats and reap the hay,                    10
We sow the apple, reap the worm,
We tread the worm and reap the turn:
Too much, too much for us this thought,
With much too much exertion fraught;
In faith we get the garden dug—                        15
And what do we reap—we reap the bug,
In goodly faith we plant the seed,
Tomorrow morn we reap the weed.

SARAH BINKS (PAUL HIEBERT, b. 1892)

## VANCOUVER LIGHTS

About me the night     moonless     wimples the mountains
wraps ocean     land     air     and mounting
sucks at the stars     The city     throbbing below
webs the sable peninsula     The golden
strands overleap the seajet     by bridge and buoy          5
vault the shears of the inlet     climb the woods
toward me     falter     and halt     Across to the firefly
haze of a ship on the gulf's erased horizon
roll the lambent spokes of a lighthouse

Through the feckless years we have come to the time         10
when to look on this quilt of lamps is a troubling delight
Welling from Europe's bog     through Africa flowing
and Asia     drowning the lonely lumes on the oceans
tiding up over Halifax     now to this winking
outpost comes flooding the primal ink                      15

On this mountain's brutish forehead with terror of space
I stir     of the changeless night and the stark ranges
of nothing     pulsing down from beyond and between

---

*wimples* (l.1): veils.
*sable* (l.4): black, dark.
*lambent* (l.9): moving lightly over a surface, as a flame.
*feckless* (l.10): useless, ineffective.
*lumes* (l.13): lights.
*primal* (l.15): primeval, from earliest times.

the fragile planets    We are a spark beleaguered
by darkness    this twinkle we make in a corner of emptiness    20
how shall we utter our fear that the black Experimentress
will never in the range of her microscope find it?    Our Phoebus
himself is a bubble that dries on Her slide    while the Nubian
wears for an evening's whim a necklace of nebulae

Yet we must speak    we the unique glowworms    25
Out of the waters and rocks of our little world
we conjured these flames    hooped these sparks
by our will    From blankness and cold we fashioned stars
to our size    and signalled Aldebaran
This must we say    whoever may be to hear us    30
if murk devour    and none weave again in gossamer:

These rays were ours
we made and unmade them    Not the shudder of continents
doused us    the moon's passion    nor crash of comets
In the fathomless heat of our dwarfdom    our dream's combustion
we contrived the power    the blast that snuffed us    35
No one bound Prometheus    Himself he chained
and consumed his own bright liver    O stranger
Plutonian    descendant    or beast in the stretching night—
there was light    40

EARLE BIRNEY (b. 1904)


## DOVER BEACH

The sea is calm tonight,
The tide is full, the moon lies fair
Upon the straits;—on the French coast the light

---

*beleaguered* (l.19): besieged, surrounded.
*Phoebus* (l.22): (Apollo) Greek god of the sun.
*Nubian* (l.23): a native of Nubia, once a country in Africa.
*nebulae* (l.24): small, bright clouds of particles and gas visible at night.
*Aldebaran* (l.29): brightest star in the constellation Taurus; from the Arabic
    word meaning "follower."
*gossamer* (l.31): fine cobwebs spun by small spiders.
*Prometheus* (l.36): a Greek demi-god, Prometheus was the son of the Titan
    Iapetus. He made the first man out of clay, and stole fire from the gods
    to further benefit mankind. For punishment Zeus chained him to a
    mountain peak in the Caucasus, and his liver was consumed each day by a
    vulture. As Prometheus was immortal, it always grew back.
*Plutonian* (l.39): of the Greek god Pluto, Lord of the underworld.

Gleams and is gone; the cliffs of England stand,
Glimmering and vast, out in the tranquil bay.                    5
Come to the window, sweet is the night-air!

Only, from the long line of spray
Where the sea meets the moon-blanched land,
Listen! you hear the grating roar
Of pebbles which the waves draw back, and fling,                10
At their return, up the high strand,
Begin, and cease, and then again begin,
With tremulous cadence slow, and bring
The eternal note of sadness in.

Sophocles long ago                                              15
Heard it on the Aegean, and it brought
Into his mind the turbid ebb and flow
Of human misery; we
Find also in the sound a thought,
Hearing it by this distant northern sea.                        20

The Sea of Faith
Was once, too, at the full, and round earth's shore
Lay like the folds of a bright girdle furled.
But now I only hear
Its melancholy, long, withdrawing roar,                         25
Retreating, to the breath
Of the night-wind, down the vast edges drear
And naked shingles of the world.

Ah, love, let us be true
To one another! for the world, which seems                      30
To lie before us like a land of dreams,
So various, so beautiful, so new,
Hath really neither joy, nor love, nor light,
Nor certitude, nor peace, nor help for pain;
And we are here as on a darkling plain                          35
Swept with confused alarms of struggle and flight,
Where ignorant armies clash by night.

MATTHEW ARNOLD (1822-1888)

---

*strand* (l.11): beach.
*tremulous cadence* (l.13): terms from music: rising and falling rhythm.
*Sophocles* (l.15): a Greek playwright of the 5th century B.C.. Many of his
    plays show a solitary person heroically resisting the evils of his time and
    circumstances.

---

# PEOPLE AND PLACES: QUESTIONS

## A. People

### Rose's Mother Was Not Good at Keeping House (p. 62)

1. Did Rose's mother have some supernatural power, or was there another explanation for the events described in the poem?
2. Summarize the main point of each stanza to see how the thought of the poem develops.
3. What meanings are suggested by the final stanza?
4. Give one word that you think best describes the tone° of this poem. Give reasons for your choice.

### Before Two Portraits of My Mother (p. 63)

1. What mixed emotions does the speaker feel?
2. How would you explain this confusion of feelings?
3. Why did the poet divide the poem into stanzas as he did?
4. What common child-parent experience does the poem express?

### Father (p. 64)

1. State what you think is the main point or topic of each stanza of the poem.
2. How has the speaker's father changed in his old age? In what ways is he the same?
3. What did the speaker learn about life from his father? Give reasons to support your answer.

### Grandfather (p. 65)

1. Paraphrase° the poem by writing a short character sketch of Grandfather. Examine the stanza divisions to help you in the sketch.
2. What personal qualities of Grandfather are most emphasized in the poem? How are these emphasized?
3. What ironies° were present in Grandfather's death?
4. Compare and contrast the mother, the father and the grandfather of the poems by Nelligan (p. 63), Zieroth (p. 64), and Bowering respectively.
5. What themes° about people can be found in the poems?

## Jim Lovenzanna (p. 66)

1. What does the story Lovenzanna told about Nick reveal about Lovenzanna himself?
2. In what way was Lovenzanna's death ironic?
3. What seems to be Mrs. Lovenzanna's feeling? Why do you think she felt that way?
4. Why are the stanza divisions placed where they are?

## Annabel Lee (p. 68)

1. Examine the rhyming words in each stanza. What rhyme° recurs many times? What does this repetition add to the poem?
2. According to the speaker, why was Annabel Lee taken from him?
3. What hint is given in stanza 4 about the real reasons she may have been taken?
4. How did their love conquer death and their enemies?
5. What elements of a classic love story are there in this poem? That is, how is this story like many other love stories?

## The Cannibal Flea (p. 69)

1. Compare and contrast this poem with *Annabel Lee* (p. 68). How are the rhymes and stanza divisions similar? What other similarities and differences do you find?
2. What are some of the sources of humor in this poem? Give examples of each.

## Canadians (p. 71)

1. Why do you think the poet chose the stanza divisions she has made?
2. Why is Canada "a country too wide to be single in"?
3. Why do you think the speaker° tells the Fathers of Confederation, don't "look so surprised"?
4. What are some features which the poem suggests are uniquely Canadian?
5. List some features that you think make Canada and Canadians unique. Try to work your ideas into a poem.

# B. Places

### In the Forest (p. 73)
1. How does the speaker feel about the forest?
2. What gives him this feeling?
3. What is your impression of the speaker of the poem? Is he foolish or does he have reason to feel as he does?
4. Make a list of the words that express the speaker's feelings about the forest.

### Morning on the Lièvre (p. 75)
1. What is the overall feeling of this poem?
2. List the most striking sights and sounds the speaker experiences.
3. What contrasts are there in the poem? What do you think is the purpose of these contrasts?
4. Both *Morning on the Lièvre* and *In the Forest* (p. 73) describe an experience in nature. How are the descriptions in the poems different? How do you account for these differences?

### The Winter Lakes (p. 77)
1. A descriptive poem such as this usually has one main overall emotion. What is the emotion of this poem? How is that emotion created? Support your answer with references to the poem.
2. The word "death" occurs three times in the poem. List other words in the poem that can be associated with death (e.g. dying, white, silence).
3. Besides death in the figurative° sense, people who enter the region risk death. What dangers to human life are described in the poem?

### My Garden (p. 77)
"Sarah Binks, the Sweet Songstress of Saskatchewan," was created by humorist Paul Hiebert. Her poems are purposely bad and are used by Hiebert to satirize° poems about nature.
1. What are some of the ridiculously bad images in the poem?
2. What are some other features that stand out as particularly bad?
3. What aspects of poems about nature is this poem making fun of or satirizing?

### Vancouver Lights (p. 78)
1. Reread the poem noting the use of capital letters and spaces to mark divisions in the thoughts. State the main idea of each stanza.
2. What human accomplishment does this poem celebrate?

3. Of what importance does the speaker feel this accomplishment was?
4. What is the theme of the poem? Support your answer with references to the poem.

### Dover Beach (p. 79)

1. Each stanza contains a main thought in the development of the poem. Give a short paraphrase of each stanza for a summary of the literal° meaning of the poem.
2. Describe the situation in which the poem might have been spoken.
3. What disturbs the speaker about the world he sees? What contrasts does he see?
4. What is the cause of these troubles?
5. What alone can overcome these troubles?

# 5 NATURE AND INVENTION

## Exploring Meaning: Unity

A POEM'S UNITY° is the way in which all its kinds of meaning hold together. In a good poem, the form°, the sense, the emotion, the tone and the intention all go together to create an effect on the reader. All of these effects unite to help the poet achieve his or her purpose. In a poor poem, we sense a certain disunity. Sometimes we are not sure if the poem is serious or humorous. Sometimes, even after several readings, we are confused. Sometimes the feeling we get does not seem to match the poet's intention. For example, the intention may appear to be to make us sad, but the rhythm° of the poem is happy and rollicking.

A good poem has unity. The emotion the poem arouses is appropriate to the statement the poem makes. The thought of the poem is developed clearly and logically. But before we can judge a poem we must understand it. Use the rest of the poems in this section to review the ideas presented so far and to hone your skills in reading and understanding.

## Nature

There are many experiences in the natural world that move us. We may be struck with awe at our first sight of the ocean. We may feel a sense of sadness while watching and hearing the waves rush against the shore. We may gasp with delight at the beauty of a sunset at sea.

Sometimes the beauty of nature reminds us of human beauty or of human imperfections. If so, we might use some natural phenomenon to symbolize a human quality. Or, we might apply a human characteristic to

85

something in nature. For example, "the cruel sea" and "icy fingers of the wind."

- How do poets use nature in these poems?
- Do they describe something in nature? If so, what is the intention?
- Do they use something in nature as a symbol?
- Do they try to explain something about human life by comparing it to something in nature?

### AN AUTUMN SONG

There is something in the autumn that is native to my blood,
Touch of manner, hint of mood;
And my heart is like a rhyme,
With the yellow and the purple and the crimson keeping time.

The scarlet of the maples can shake me like a cry                  5
Of bugles going by.
And my lonely spirit thrills
To see the frosty asters like smoke upon the hills.

There is something in October sets the gipsy blood astir:
We must rise and follow her,                                       10
When from every hill aflame
She calls and calls each vagabond by name.

BLISS CARMAN (1861-1929)

### TO AUTUMN

Season of mists and mellow fruitfulness,
    Close bosom-friend of the maturing sun;
Conspiring with him how to load and bless
    With fruit the vines that round the thatch-eves run;

---

*asters* (l.8): daisy-like flowers.
*vagabond* (l.12): a wanderer.

---

*To Autumn, thatch-eves* (l.4): edges of thatched (straw-covered) roofs.

To bend with apples the mossed cottage-trees,                    5
    And fill all fruit with ripeness to the core;
        To swell the gourd, and plump the hazel shells
    With a sweet kernel; to set budding more,
And still more, later flowers for the bees,
Until they think warm days will never cease,                    10
    For Summer has o'er-brimmed their clammy cells.

Who hath not seen thee oft amid thy store?
    Sometimes whoever seeks abroad may find
    Thee sitting careless on a granary floor,
        Thy hair soft-lifted by the winnowing wind;        15
    Or on a half-reaped furrow sound asleep,
        Drowsed with the fume of poppies, while thy hook
            Spares the next swath and all its twinèd flowers:
    And sometimes like a gleaner thou dost keep
        Steady thy laden head across a brook;              20
    Or by a cyder-press, with patient look,
        Thou watchest the last oozings hours by hours.

Where are the songs of Spring? Ay, where are they?
    Think not of them, thou hast thy music too,—
While barrèd clouds bloom the soft-dying day,              25
    And touch the stubble-plains with rosy hue;
Then in a wailful choir the small gnats mourn
    Among the river sallows, borne aloft
        Or sinking as the light wind lives or dies;
And full-grown lambs loud bleat from hilly bourn;         30
    Hedge-crickets sing; and now with treble soft
    The red-breast whistles from a garden-croft;
        And gathering swallows twitter in the skies.

JOHN KEATS (1795-1821)

---

*gourd* (l.7): the large, fleshy fruit of a climbing plant.
*gleaner* (l.19): one who gathers grain left by the reapers.
*sallows* (l.28): willows.
*bourn* (l.30): an unusual use of the word (the Oxford English dictionary
    actually says Keats was "incorrect" in the way he uses it in this poem!): it
    probably means a domain or territory.

## THE TIGER

Tiger! Tiger! burning bright
In the forests of the night,
What immortal hand or eye
Could frame thy fearful symmetry?

In what distant deeps or skies                    5
Burnt the fire of thine eyes?
On what wings dare he aspire?
What the hand dare seize the fire?

And what shoulder, and what art,
Could twist the sinews of thy heart?              10
And when thy heart began to beat,
What dread hand? and what dread feet?

What the hammer? what the chain?
In what furnace was thy brain?
What the anvil? what dread grasp                  15
Dare its deadly terrors clasp?

When the stars threw down their spears,
And watered heaven with their tears,
Did he smile his work to see?
Did he who made the Lamb make thee?               20

Tiger! Tiger! burning bright
In the forests of the night,
What immortal hand or eye
Dare frame thy fearful symmetry?

WILLIAM BLAKE (1757-1827)


## THE LAMB

Little Lamb, who made thee?
Dost thou know who made thee?
Gave thee life, and bade thee feed,
By the stream and o'er the mead;

---

*symmetry* (l.4): balanced, pleasing proportions.
*aspire* (l.7): to have ambition for something, with the connotation° of
  breathing (from Latin *aspirare*, to breathe).

---

*The Lamb, mead* (l.4): meadow.

---

Gave thee clothing of delight,                                    5
Softest clothing, woolly, bright;
Gave thee such a tender voice,
Making all the vale rejoice?
    Little Lamb, who made thee?
    Dost thou know who made thee?                             10

    Little Lamb, I'll tell thee,
    Little Lamb, I'll tell thee:
He is calléd by thy name,
For He calls Himself a Lamb,
He is meek, and He is mild;                                       15
He became a little child.
I a child, and thou a lamb,
We are calléd by His name.
    Little Lamb, God bless thee!
    Little Lamb, God bless thee!

WILLIAM BLAKE (1757-1827)


## BREAK, BREAK, BREAK

Break, break, break,
    On thy cold gray stones, O Sea!
And I would that my tongue could utter
    The thoughts that arise in me.

O well for the fisherman's boy,                                   5
    That he shouts with his sister at play!
O well for the sailor lad,
    That he sings in his boat on the bay!

And the stately ships go on
    To their haven under the hill;                               10
But O for the touch of a vanished hand,
    And the sound of a voice that is still!

Break, break, break,
    At the foot of thy crags, O Sea!

---

*vale* (l.8): a valley.
*calléd* (l.13): pronounced as two distinct syllables (call-ed).

---

*Break, Break, Break, would* (l.3): wish.
*vanished hand* (l.11): a reference to Arthur Hallam, a close friend of
    Tennyson, who died young.

But the tender grace of a day that is dead                    15
    Will never come back to me.

ALFRED LORD TENNYSON (1809-1892)


## THE BATHER'S DIRGE

Break, break, break,
    On thy cold, hard stones, O sea!
And I hope that my tongue won't utter
    The curses that rise in me.

Oh, well for the fisherman's boy,                             5
    If he likes to be soused with the spray!
Oh, well for the sailor lad,
    As he paddles about in the bay!

And the ships swim happily on,
    To their haven under the hill;                      10
But O for a clutch of that vanished hand,
    And a kick—for I'm catching a chill!

Break, break, break,
    At my poor bare feet, O sea!
But the artful scamp who has collar'd my clothes             15
    Will never come back to me.

AUTHOR UNKNOWN


## I REMEMBER THE WHITE BEAR

I remember the white bear,
With its back-body raised high;
It thought it was the only male here,
And came towards me at full speed.
    *Unaya, unaya.*                                       5

Again and again it threw me down,
But it did not lie over me,
But quickly went from me again.
It had not thought
Of meeting other males here,                                 10
And by the edge of an ice floe
It lay down calmly.
    *Unaya, unaya.*

I shall never forget the great blubber-beast;
On the firm ice I had already flayed it,                     15

When the neighbors with whom I shared the land here
Had just woken.
It was as if I had just gone to its breathing hole out there.
    *Unaya, unaya.*

There as I came across it,                                    20
And as I stood over it, it heard me,
Without scratching at the ice,
At the under edge of the firm ice to which it
    had hooked itself,
Truly it was a cunning beast—
Just as I felt sorry that I had not caught it,               25
    *Unaya, unaya,*

I caught it fast with my harpoon head,
Before it had even drawn breath!

NETSILIK ESKIMO


## L'ORIGNAL

The bull moose only a startling rod or so away from me
looked to be about nine feet long
maybe six feet above the trampled-down snow
and he would go about a thousand pounds
even though starved gaunt. He was murder-angry had eaten    5
all the undergrowth and above him all twigs and branches
within reach so that the little forest on his island was
    trimmed
evenly along the lower parts of the trees
according to the undulations of the land

This mini-skirts appearance of the island had drawn my
    curiosity                                        10
as I crossed the lake on the way home with the new axe—
to encounter the terrifying sight at close range of *l'orignal*
as the French long ago named the bull moose having never
seen so strange an animal in Europe (The Indians called
    him mongswa
from which the English took the name the twig eater)    15

The moose had probably been chased to this island
in the deep of winter. Nearby me on the lake ice lay a long-
    dead wolf

---

*L'Orignal*: the French word for moose.

(on a guess, a wolf—I hadn't seen one outside a museum or zoo)
frozen at full stretch and partly drifted over.
I figured that the moose had used the small island as a fort          20
Even after the wolves gave up and went away
the moose may have stayed browsing but the island had
    trapped him

The ice shore had become too weak for a getaway
The late winter sun heating shore rocks
had circled the island with a thin-crusted moat. I observed          25
where the starving moose had several times broken through
in trying to escape after he had eaten everything within reach
Dimly seeing me out here among pressure ridges
and water pools in the sugar snow over yard-deep ice
the moose probably took me for one of those wolves               30
so he charged

Immediately he splintered though the ice and disappeared
When he came up on a tide of icicles and water
he kept on trying to get at me slamming
the breaking ice with his forelegs. He had no horns.               35
I however was having a close look at his front hooves
until he turned around and feebly swam through ice-floes
He was a long time dragging himself up over the shore rocks.

I walked half-way around his little island
and bellied over the thin ice pushing                            40
my axe ahead of me. I didn't quite break through
and ashore quickly inexpertly cut down a poplar
pushing it inland as the moose staggered toward me
The falling treetop confronted his weak charge. The
    monster
began to nibble on the delicate twigs                            45
In March all deer are starving and weak but this one
was the prize woebegone. His bell was thin as a string
He stayed at the end of the tree and kept eating
while I managed to hack down another poplar and another
ruining our environment and probably breaking some laws          50
but there was peace between that moose and me. I worked
until I figured that he had fodder enough for break-up
when he could get off the island and swim to a mainland
forest for a fresh start. Then I crawled full length
over the weak shore ice and walked along the lake                55
in the last of the late-winter day

R.G. EVERSON (b. 1930)

# Invention

A great human talent is our ability to create. Humans can take natural objects like stones, sand, cement and water and mix them together to form concrete which we use for buildings and roads. We can also take observations of events in nature and create theories or explanations of how those things came to be. No scientist was present when the earth was formed, but many scientists have theories about how it happened.

New inventions and breakthroughs in science are usually referred to as "progress." But some people feel that although we gain something with each new invention, we lose something as well:

- Is each new scientific or technological breakthrough a benefit to humans?
- If harm comes from science and technology, is the harm in the invention or in the way humans use it?
- Have some inventions enabled humans to reach beyond themselves, to achieve a higher state of being for all humanity?
- We live in a scientific era. Are we on the brink of a wonderful new age, or are we on the edge of disaster?


## JULIETTE AND HER FRIENDS VISIT CHERRY BEACH

cables and cameras and lights and don't foget—yellow—is
  julie's colour and we want all the girls in dresses not jeans and
  tell the men we want a fight and we don't want anyone hurt
  and watch the language this is a ladies show

but we want the truth about the beatings but we want to catch a   5
  robbery on camera but we don't want any blood but we want
  to show the ladies in the audience how an arrest is made on
  the street but please watch the language this is a ladies show

if you see a pusher we want to photograph the transaction if 10
  there's a high speed chase we want our cameras to be there
  with you all the way if you get hurt we'll certainly compensate
  you and if in your work you can find us a setting for one of
  julie's songs that would be just great

HANS JEWINSKI (b. 1946)

---

*Juliette*: a glamorous blond singer who starred on CBC television for many
years.
*Cherry Beach*: a beach on the Toronto waterfront near the downtown area.

## SOUTH VIEWED BY NORTH AMERICAN ESKIMO

South
Is the world which is a living thing itself.
It controls its people and the people are prisoners.
It is a machine world.
It is not *South* itself,                                         5
it is people
they are too concerned with the things they own or their
    country
(formerly an Amerindian nation, now know as NORTH
    AMERICA)
that they even forget their fellow members or other people.
They fight each other like brainless dogs,                        10
rather than helping each other which *they should.*
For one little example among others—
In World War II Canadians
didn't trade their wheat to other countries but instead
they burned it                                                    15
because they wanted to keep the price up.
I would call this "A Wild Democracy" or "The Go Go
Democracy"
just the same so-called "The wild tribes of Africa".
To you I am using dirty words                                     20
to me they are simply funny words.
I think I will never hate individual cultures or try to convert
    them or brainwash them.
I happen to be in the family which some of the people call
Mongoliform,
and here is one of my experiences or part of my "education"
    I would prefer to call it.                   25
In all the years of being in the south I never miss the good
movies,
and some of them are war movies like Japanese war movies.
Of course, there are always breathtaking parts in these
movies, and the fellows sitting near me usually get wild,        30
wilder when they could sit beside me.
(Instead of enjoying the breathtaking part I watch
the fellow to see whether he takes his knife out of his
pocket or opens it already.)
Talking about Mongoliform business, an Eskimo friend
    and I                                      35
were driving down to United States
to see a friend in Ithaca, N.Y.
We happened to carry only social insurance cards with us,

and boy
we spent two and a half hours on the damned border     40
trying to say that we were Eskimos.

P. KOOLERK


## I LIKE TO SEE IT
## LAP THE MILES

I like to see it lap the Miles—
And lick the Valleys up—
And stop to feed itself at Tanks—
and then—prodigious step

Around a Pile of Mountains—                              5
And supercilious peer
In Shanties—by the sides of Roads—
And then a Quarry pare

To fit its Ribs
And crawl between                                       10
Complaining all the while
In horrid—hooting stanza—
Then chase itself down Hill—

And neigh like Boanerges—
Then—punctual as a Star                                 15
Stop—docile and omnipotent
At its own stable door—

EMILY DICKINSON (1830-1886)


## HIGH FLIGHT

O, I have slipped the surly bonds of earth
    And danced the skies on laughter-silvered wings.
Sunward I've climbed and joined the tumbling mirth
    Of sun-split clouds—and done a hundred things

---

*prodigious* (l.4): huge; also wonderful, marvellous.
*supercilious* (l.6): arrogant; proud and contemptuous.
*pare* (l.8): cut or trim.
*Boanerges* (l.13): name given by Christ to his apostles James and John, who
    were brothers. The word is from Aramaic, meaning "sons of thunder."
*docile* (l.15): obedient; easy to manage.

You have not dreamed of—wheeled and soared and swung 5
   High in the sunlit silence. Hovering there,
I've chased the shouting wind along and flung
   My eager craft through footless halls of air.
Up, up the long delirious, burning blue
   I've topped the wind-swept heights with easy grace      10
Where never lark, or even eagle flew,
   And, while with silent, lifting mind I've trod
The high untrespassed sanctity of space,
   Put out my hand and touched the face of God.

JOHN GILLESPIE MAGEE (1922-1940)


## WHEN I HEARD THE LEARN'D ASTRONOMER

When I heard the learn'd astronomer,
When the proofs, the figures, were ranged in columns
   before me,
When I was shown the charts and diagrams, to add, divide,
   and measure them,
When I sitting heard the astronomer where he lectured
   with much applause in the lecture-room,
How soon unaccountable I became tired and sick,      5
Till rising and gliding out I wander'd off by myself,
In the mystical moist night-air, and from time to time,
Look'd up in perfect silence at the stars.

WALT WHITMAN (1819-1892)


## O EARTH, TURN!

The little blessed Earth that turns
Does so on its own concerns
As though it weren't my home at all;
It turns me winter, summer, fall
Without a thought of me.      5

I love the slightly flattened sphere,
Its restless, wrinkled crust's my here,

---

*footless halls of air* (l.8): imaginary corridors in the skies where no one has
   ever been before.

---

*When I Heard the Learn'd Astronomer, unaccountable* (l.5): unaccountably
   for no reason.

Its slightly wobbling spin's my now
But not my why and not my how:
My why and how are me.                                    10

GEORGE JOHNSTON (b. 1913)

---

# NATURE AND INVENTION: QUESTIONS

---

## A. Nature

**An Autumn Song (p. 87)**
1. What emotions does autumn evoke in the speaker?
2. What relationships does the speaker sense between himself and autumn?
3. How does the rhythm° of the poem help to express its meaning and to create feeling and tone? Give examples to illustrate your answer.
4. What season stirs your emotions most? Jot down a few ideas about that season and how it affects you. Shape your ideas into a poem.

**To Autumn (p. 87)**
1. What images° of autumn does the poem present?
2. Why are these images appropriate?
3. Compare this poem with *An Autumn Song* (p. 87). How are the feelings and tone different? What features of the poems create these differences?
4. How does the poet's experience of autumn compare with your own?

**The Tiger (p. 89)**
1. The first and last stanzas provide a framework for the rest of the poem. How are the first and last stanzas different from each other? How do you explain this difference?
2. In what sense could the tiger be "burning bright"?
3. Stanzas 2, 3 and 4 each describe one feature of the tiger. What are they?
4. The first four stanzas ask variations of one question. The last two stanzas ask two other questions. What questions does the poem ask? What answers are suggested by the feeling and tone of the poem?

## The Lamb (p. 89)

1. How is the first stanza related to the second?
2. Compare this poem with *The Tiger* (p. 89).
   a. In what ways are they alike?
   b. What are some differences between them in
      —images and figurative language°?
      —rhythm?
3. How are the two poems different in tone? How does the poet create these effects?
4. What statements are made about the Creator in these two poems? What two views of nature are presented?

## Break, Break, Break (p. 90)

1. What three references to speaking are made in the first three stanzas? How do these references give meaning° to the poem?
2. What words are repeated several times in the poem?
3. Do you think this poem is an effective statement of the speaker's grief? Give reasons for your opinion.
4. Compare this poem with *The Bather's Dirge* (p. 91).

## The Bather's Dirge (p. 91)

1. Compare this poem with Tennyson's *Break, Break Break* (p. 90).
   a. To what extent has the poet of the parody kept the rhythm and rhyme° of the original?
   b. Besides the final twist, in what other ways is the parody° different from the original?
   c. How has the phrase "vanished hand" taken on new meaning in the parody?

## I Remember the White Bear (p. 91)

1. For which do you feel sympathy, the bear or the man? Why?
2. What view of the relationship between nature and humanity does this poem present?
3. How does the view of that relationship as expressed in this poem compare with your own?
4. Compare this poem with *The Tiger* (p. 89) and *The Lamb* (p. 89) written by the English poet William Blake before 1800. What similarities in thought or theme can you find in the poems?

## L'Orignal (p. 92)

1. How is the relationship between human beings and nature different in

this poem from that shown in *I Remember the White Bear* (p. 91)?
2. What do you think is the theme of this poem? Support your opinion with references to the poem.
3. Is this poem an effective and unified statement of the theme? Give reasons for your opinion.

# B. Invention

**Juliette and Her Friends Visit Cherry Beach (p. 94)**
1. Who might be the speaker in this poem? To whom might he or she be speaking? What might the situation be?
2. What is revealed about the speaker's character?
3. Who or what might the speaker be used to represent?

**South Viewed by North American Eskimo (p. 96)**
1. What criticisms of the south does the speaker make?
2. How does the tone of the second stanza differ from that of the first? What lines mark this change of tone?
3. Is the episode at the border an appropriate conclusion to the poem? Give reasons for your answser.

**I Like to See It Lap the Miles (p. 97)**
1. What is being described in the poem? To what is that object compared?
2. Besides liking the machine, what else is conveyed about the speaker's feelings toward it?
3. Note the punctuation in the poem. How many sentences does the poem contain? How is punctuation, or the lack of it, used to give a feeling of motion? How is that feeling of motion stopped?
4. Do you think this poem is an effective statement about the machine it describes? Give reasons for your answer.

**High Flight (p. 97)**
1. What feeling is conveyed in this poem? What words and expressions help to create that feeling?
2. What feeling does the speaker express in the last few lines of the poem? How is this feeling different from that of the first part of the poem?

3. If this poem were to be divided into two parts, where would you make the division? Why?
4. Do you think the poem is an effective description of flight?

### When I Heard the Learn'd Astronomer (p. 98)

1. What is the speaker's view of astronomy? What was it about the astronomer's lecture that bothered the speaker?
2. The word "unaccountable" (l.5) is related in meaning to the idea expressed in line 3. How does this make the word especially effective?
3. Why is the word "mystical" well-chosen?
4. Why do you think the poet started the first four lines with the same words?
5. How is the feeling in the last three lines different from the feeling in the rest of the poem? How do words, sounds and rhythm contribute to those feelings?

### O Earth, Turn! (p. 98)

1. How does the speaker see his place on the earth?
2. What is meant by saying the earth is "my here" and "my now/But not my why and not my how"?
3. What is meant by the last line?
4. State your interpretation of the sense, the feeling, the tone and the intention of this poem.

# 6 ANYTHING AND EVERY-THING

Poems deal with the full range of human experiences. Often, a simple experience represents or suggests something much larger. Poets are always alert and open to their experiences, finding meanings that are often overlooked.

Simple actions or objects can have significant meanings. Think of what a hug means when you are lonely or depressed. Do you have souvenirs from places you have visited? Why did you bring these things back? Do you have keepsakes such as toys or articles of clothing that you have kept since your childhood? Why have you kept these things? Are there certain sounds, or scents, or kinds of days that remind you of certain people, or places, or times in your life?

All of these simple things can become the inspiration or starting point for a poem. They can become symbols around which to focus a powerful experience. In the poems that follow, notice how the poets have made use of simple objects to represent much deeper meanings.

Read these poems for enjoyment, but remember that a good poem should be read several times. To enjoy a poem is to understand its subtler aspects which may be lost in one quick reading.

This grouping is the final one in part one of this book, and, as its title suggests, it ranges widely. The poems in it will allow you to explore all the kinds of meaning discussed throughout this first part of *The Poet's Craft*.

## THE RYANS AND THE PITTMANS
## (OR: WE'LL RANT AND WE'LL ROAR LIKE TRUE
## NEWFOUNDLANDERS)

We'll rant and we'll roar like true Newfoundlanders,
　　We'll rant and we'll roar on deck and below,
Until we see bottom inside the two sunkers
　　When straight through the channel to Toslow we'll go.

I'm a son of a sea-cook, and a cook in a trader;　　　　　　　5
　　I can dance, I can sing, I can reef the main-boom,
I can handle a jigger, and cuts a big figure
　　Whenever I gets in a boat's standing room.

If the voyage is good, then this fall I will do it;
　　I wants two pound ten for a ring and the priest,　　　　10
A couple o' dollars for clane shirt and collars,
　　And a handful o'coppers to make up a feast.

There's plump little Polly, her name is Goldsworthy;
　　There's John Coady's Kitty, and Mary Tibbo;
There's Clara from Bruley, and young Martha Foley,　　　　15
　　But the nicest of all is my girl in Toslow.

Farewell and adieu to ye fair ones of Valen,
　　Farewell and adieu to ye girls in the Cove;
I'm bound to the Westward, to the wall with the hole in,
　　I'll take her from Toslow the wild world to rove.　　　　20

Farewell and adieu to ye girls of St. Kyran's,
　　Of Paradise and Presque, Big and Little Bona,
I'm bound unto Toslow to marry sweet Biddy,
　　And if I don't do so, I'm afraid of her da.

I've bought me a house from Katherine Davis,　　　　　　25
　　A twenty-pound bed from Jimmy McGrath;
I'll get me a settle, a pot and a kettle;
　　Then I'll be ready for Biddy—Hurrah!

I brought in the Ino this spring from the city
　　Some rings and gold brooches for the girls in the Bay;　　30
I bought me a case-pipe—they call it a meerschaum—
　　It melted like butter upon a hot day.

I went to a dance one night at Fox Harbour;
　　There were plenty of girls, so nice as you'd wish,

---

*jigger* (l.7): a small sail.

There was one pretty maiden a-chawing of frankgum,        35
  Just like a young kitten a-gnawing fresh fish.

Then here is a health to the girls of Fox Harbour,
  Of Oderin and Presque, Crabbes Hole and Bruley.
Now let ye be jolly, don't be melancholy,
  I can't marry all, or in chokey I'd be.        40

     H.W. LE MESSURIER

## MACDONALD'S CAMP

1. One evening last fall when we felt well inclined
   We hired with D. A. MacDonald to work at the pine.
   The place he put us was rougher than blazes;
   It was down at the new base among the hard cases.

REFRAIN
*Singing fal a-ler-ler-dle, il-der-dle, i-lay.*

2. Here's for D.A. MacDonald, he was a devil to trot.     5
   He brought bread seven miles, and he got it here hot.
   When we sat down to dinner we thought we had none,
   But the boss he arrived there before we got done.

3. Here's for our cook, he was as good as gold.
   He left his old father when fourteen years old.     10
   He hired at D. A. MacDonald for to do what he could—
   For to score at the loaf and to chop at the wood.

4. Here's for James Proudfoot comes next in our song.
   If Jimmy don't do better he won't be here long.
   At breaking saw handles is Jimmy's delight,     15
   For to get into the shanty long before it's night.

5. Here is for Bernie Knott, he's our swamper you know.
   He works very steady but devilish slow.
   He cuts his stumps high and he trims his knots long,
   And tell him to do better, he never lets on.     20

6. Here is for young Charlie Proudfoot comes next in our song.
   He contracted for a cedar that did not last long.
   He got three cents a post, and I think he cut seven.
   Success to you, Charlie, I wish you eleven!

7. Here's for Malcolm Montgomery, he roams far and
        wide.     25
   He spied some long tamarack down by the lakeside.
   The place this timber grew it must have been forgotten,
   For Malcolm he swears that the half of it's rotten.

8. Here's for Joe Townsend, a fine lad is he.
   He drives a gay team, and you all know they're free.     30
   He shoves on the big load, and you hear his whip crack,
   And away goes the whiffletrees over their back.

9. Here is to Jack Caldwell, the next in our song.
   At rolling the logs he is no use at all.
   When he meets a big log he gets a pain in his back,     35
   And then he is ready to ask for the *sack*.

AUTHOR UNKNOWN

---

*swamper* (l.17): person who fells trees and clears away undergrowth to
   make a logging road.
*tamarack* (l.26): indian name for a type of pine tree.

## CANADIAN RAILROAD TRILOGY

There was a time in this fair land when the railroad did not
run,
When the wild majestic mountains stood alone against the
sun.
Long before the white man, and long before the wheel
When the green dark forest was too silent to be real.

But time has no beginnings and hist'ry has no bounds,      5
As to this verdant country they came from all around.
They sailed upon her waterways and they walked the forests
tall,
Built the mines, mills and factories for the good of us all.

And when the young man's fancy was turning in the spring,
The railroad men grew restless for to hear the hammers
ring.                                                      10
Their minds were overflowing with the visions of their day
And many a fortune won and lost and many a debt to pay.

For they looked in the future and what did they see
They saw an iron road running from the sea to the sea.
Bringin' the goods to a young growin' land                 15
All up from the seaports and into their hands.

Bring in the workers and bring up the rails
We gotta lay down the tracks and tear up the trails.
Open her heart let the life-blood flow
Gotta get on our way 'cause we're movin' too slow.         20
Get on our way 'cause we're movin' too slow.

Behind the blue Rockies the sun is declinin'
The stars they come stealin' at the close of the day.
Across the wide prairie our loved ones lie sleeping
Beyond the dark forest in a place far away.                25
We are the plough-boys who work upon the railway
Swingin' our hammers in the bright blazin' sun.
Livin' on stew and drinkin' bad whisky
Layin' down track 'til the long days are done
Yeah, bendin' our backs 'til the railroad is done.         30

Now the song of the future has been sung,
All the battles have been won,

---

*verdant* (l.6): green, fertile.

On the mountain tops we stand,
All the world at our command,
We have opened up the soil                                    35
With our tear-drops and our toil.

There was a time in this fair land when the railroad did not
    run,
When the wild majestic mountains stood alone against the sun.
Long before the white man, and long before the wheel
When the green dark forest was too silent to be real.          40
When the green dark forest was too silent to be real,
And many are the dead men too silent to be real.

GORDON LIGHTFOOT (b. 1939)


## SECOND DEGREE BURNS

My friend at the party said:
You'll get second-degree burns
If you keep sneaking through the fire

I wasn't sneaking
I was hovering with my hand                                    5
And anyway
It wasn't fire
But a candle

A candle involves fire, but
So does a hand                                                10

Trees involve fire
Streetcars involve fire

We all have second-degree burns
And they hurt but the hurt doesn't matter

The living flame of the world is what matters                 15
The fire is edible, and now

GWENDOLYN MacEWEN (b. 1941)


## THE CRUMBLING WALL

A crumbling wall
is a good thing,

it saves a city,
this kind of city,

pushing itself north                                    5
wall against new wall.

The foundation
is crumbling, that

is the only way
a community can build.                                 10

Let the bricks
fall out. A broken

wall is a thing of
beauty, for a certain

time. Joy does not                                     15
last forever. It

requires change, it
must crumble to remain.

GEORGE BOWERING (b. 1935)


## REFLECTING SUNGLASSES

Circles of sky
and storefronts in my face—
look through me:
lattice of moving air
chrome    sunburst    faces—                           5
I'm a see-through woman
proof enough of
the proposition that we're all
mostly
empty space.                                           10
I swing along carrying
tunnels of vision
through the imaginary fabric
of my brain.
Lean closer and you'll see                             15
you looking out
from me.

PAT LOWTHER (1935-1975)

## UNEMPLOYMENT

The chrome lid of the coffee pot
twists off, and the glass knob rinsed.
Lift out the assembly, dump
the grounds out. Wash the pot and
fill with water, put everything back with            5
fresh grounds and snap the top down.
Plug in again and wait.

Unemployment is also
a great snow deep around the house
choking the street, and the City.            10
Nothing moves. Newspaper photographs
show the traffic backed up for miles.
Going out to shovel the walk
I think how in a few days the sun will clear this.
No one will know I worked here.            15

This is like whatever I do.
How strange that so magnificent a thing as a body
with its twinges, its aches
should have all that chemistry, that bulk
the intricate electrical brain            20
subjected to something as tiny
as buying a postage stamp.
Or selling it.

Or waiting.

TOM WAYMAN (b. 1945)


## THE BLIND MEN AND THE ELEPHANT
*A Hindoo Fable*

It was six men of Indostan
    To learning much inclined,
Who went to see the Elephant
    (Though all of them were blind),
That each by observation            5
    Might satisfy his mind.

---

*Indostan* (l.1): Hindustan.

The *First* approached the Elephant,
  And happening to fall
Against his broad and sturdy side,
  At once began to bawl:        10
"God bless me! but the Elephant
  Is very like a wall!"

The *Second*, feeling of the tusk,
  Cried, "Ho! what have we here
So very round and smooth and sharp?      15
  To me 'tis mighty clear
This wonder of an Elephant
  Is very like a spear!"

The *Third* approached the animal,
  And happening to take        20
The squirming trunk within his hands,
  Thus boldly up and spake:
"I see," quoth he, "the Elephant
  Is very like a snake!"

The *Fourth* reached out an eager hand,     25
  And felt about the knee.
"What most this wondrous beast is like
  Is mighty plain," quoth he;
" 'Tis clear enough the Elephant
  Is very like a tree!"        30

The *Fifth* who chanced to touch the ear,
  Said: "E'en the blindest man
Can tell what this resembles most;
  Deny the fact who can,
This marvel of an Elephant        35
  Is very like a fan!"

The *Sixth* no sooner had begun
  About the beast to grope,
Then, seizing on the swinging tail
  That fell within his scope,       40
"I see," quoth he, "the Elephant
  Is very like a rope!"

And so these men of Indostan
  Disputed loud and long,
Each in his own opinion        45
  Exceeding stiff and strong,
Though each was partly in the right,
  And all were in the wrong!

*Moral*

So oft in theologic wars,
    The disputants, I ween,                                    50
Rail on in utter ignorance
    Of what each other mean,
*And prate about an Elephant*
*Not one of them has seen!*

JOHN GODFREY SAXE (1816-1887)

# ANYTHING AND EVERYTHING: QUESTIONS

**The Ryans and the Pittmans (p. 105)**
1. What human experiences does the song celebrate?
2. Why do you think the song includes the names of so many people and places?
3. Compare and contrast this song with *The Banks of Newfoundland* (p. 9). Consider theme, feeling and other points you consider important.

**MacDonald's Camp (p. 106)**
1. Why are the people named in the song?
2. In what setting might the song be sung?
3. How is this song like *The Ryans and the Pittmans* (p. 105)?
4. What were the intentions of such songs?
5. Compare this song with *Lost Jimmy Whelan* (p. 28). In your comparison consider as many kinds of meaning° as you can.

**Canadian Railroad Trilogy (p. 108)**
1. Why are the first and last stanzas the same except for one line? Why do you think that line has been added?
2. What seems to be the speaker's feeling about the building of the railway? Give reasons for your answer.
3. What might have been the intention of this song?

---

*theologic wars* (1.49): arguments about religion.
*ween* (1.50): think; believe.
*prate* (1.53): talk idly, chatter.

4. This is a modern folk song. Compare it with the older folk songs in this section. What similarities and differences do you find?

### Second Degree Burns (p. 109)
1. In what way do a hand, a tree and streetcars involve fire?
2. In what sense do "we all have second-degree burns"?
3. Of what importance is the fire to the speaker?
4. What is the dominant tone of the poem?
5. What seems to be the speaker's view of life? Support your answer with references to the poem.
6. Do you agree with that view? What in your own experience do you think has shaped your view of life?

### The Crumbling Wall (p. 109)
1. What theme or broader meaning does the wall suggest to the speaker?
2. What seems to be the tone of this poem?
3. Explain the meaning of the last sentence of the poem.
4. Does this poem have unity°? Give reasons for your opinion.

### Reflecting Sunglasses (p. 110)
1. What thoughts do the sunglasses arouse in the speaker?
2. Explain these expressions:
   • "I'm a see-through woman";
   • "carrying/tunnels of vision/through the imaginary fabric/of my brain."
3. Think of some common item of clothing or apparel that you are familiar with. Use that item as the poet has used sunglasses to suggest other meanings. What could the item you choose symbolize or represent?

### Unemployment (p. 112)
1. What feeling is expressed in the poem? How has unemployment affected the speaker?
2. Explain the expression, "Unemployment is also/a great snow deep around the house/choking the street".
3. What concrete items symbolize the speaker's feelings?
4. Do you think this poem is an effective expression of the feelings an unemployed person would have? Give reasons for your opinion.

### The Blind Men and the Elephant (p. 112)
1. What does the poem suggest about the causes of religious arguments?

2. What seems to be the speaker's opinion about religious arguments? Do you agree with this opinion?
3. How is humor created in the poem?
4. Notice the subtitle. In what ways is the poem a fable?
5. If this poem were to be written today, what object might be chosen instead of an elephant? Work out some ideas that could be used in an up-dated version of this poem. You might like to try writing a poem using your ideas.

# PART II

## THE POET'S CRAFT

# 1 HOW POETS SPEAK

## Introduction

The words of the poet and the words you and I use in everyday conversation are alike in many ways. We often use words to mean something different from their literal, dictionary meanings. For example, we say, "the sun rises in the east." But we know that the sun does not rise or set. The earth rotates on its axis and turns our part of the world into the sun's rays or out of them. We also speak of such things as "rich" farmland, of a ship "threading" its way through an ice "field" and so on.

We often want to express an emotion or to give special emphasis to our words. We might use slang for this purpose. For example, "These kids are driving me up the wall!" is more emphatic than, "The children are misbehaving." We use language, then, to suggest more meanings than the literal or dictionary meanings of the words. The poet makes frequent use of language for such purposes, but the poet's language is fresher, more original and more forceful than most slang.

Throughout Part One of this book, there are comments on the many kinds of meaning that poetry contains. It is through the careful use of words that poets control these kinds of meaning so that readers are able to re-create in their minds the experience a given poet is discussing. There is no such thing as a "poetic" word. Do not think that the biggest, the most unusual or the most flowery words are more poetic than any others. The most ordinary words can be used effectively in poems. Their value depends on how well they achieve the poet's purpose. In this chapter we will examine several of the factors which influence the poet's choice of words: connotation and denotation, figurative language, irony, imagery and symbol and allusion.

119

# Connotation and Denotation

What are the differences between the four descriptions below?
- my paternal parent's Rolls Royce;
- my dad's car;
- my old man's heap;
- my pop's jalopy.

Each description has the same denotation°. Each describes an automobile owned by the speaker's father. But the words used in each description create different reactions or carry different meanings. Each description has a different connotation°. What suggestions are there in each description about the car, the speaker's feelings about his or her father, the speaker, the audience (i.e. the person(s) spoken to) and the situation in which the words are spoken?

Poets use ordinary language, but they use it with precision and choose words with multiple meanings to suggest not only literal meanings (sense) but also emotion. Because poets are limited in the number of words they can use in a given poem, each word must be carefully chosen to create the specific emotion, to emphasize the particular point and to define the precise meaning that they intend.

Many words have more than one denotation. That is, the dictionary will give several literal meanings for the word. For example, the Gage *Dictionary of Canadian English* lists 44 meanings for the word "run" used as a verb and 22 meanings for the same word used as a noun. The only way to decide which of the many meanings a word may have in a particular poem is to examine the context in which the word is used. For example, if the context of the word "run" contains such other words as "candidate," "election," "office," and "vote," you can already make a good guess as to which meaning it has. If, on the other hand, the context has such words as "color," "sweater," and "wash," you can infer a very different meaning for "run."

The connotations of a word are even more numerous because they are the result of all the past expriences we have had with what that word signifies. Connotations often carry most of the emotional meanings of words. So the reader must use not only the words, but also the feeling, the tone and the apparent intention of the poem to decide which of many connotations are appropriate.

• **Being Aware of Connotations**
1. We might say, "The king drank a glass of red wine." The poet says, the king sat "Drinking the blood-red wine." What are the connotations of the poet's description?
2. We might say, "I made a serious mistake and it ended our relationship." What are the connotations of the poet's saying, "The fault was grave!"
3. What are some of the connotations of the italicized words in these excerpts?
   a) The poet says he does not fear death, but looks forward to it, for he will regain peace and love. The last line of the poem is, "And with God be the *rest!*"
   b) The poet wants these words engraved on his tombstone:
      "*Home* is the *sailor*, home from the *sea*,
      And the *hunter* home from the *hill*."
   c) In two different poems, we have similar words used. One says the soldiers "*creep* to death;" another says a dying brother "*crawls* toward death."
   d) A man sees "An *angel* writing in a book of *gold*."

## FIRE AND ICE

Some say the world will end in fire;
Some say in ice.
From what I've tasted of desire
I hold with those who favor fire.
But if it had to perish twice,                                    5
I think I know enough of hate
To know that for destruction ice
Is also great
And would suffice.

ROBERT FROST (1874-1963)

## Questions
1. The meaning of this poem rests largely on the connotations of the two nouns in the title. What are these connotations?
2. What other words in the poem are associated with fire? Which are associated with ice? What are the associations?

## NAMING OF PARTS

Today we have naming of parts. Yesterday,
We had daily cleaning. And tomorrow morning,
We shall have what to do after firing. But today,
Today we have naming of parts. Japonica
Glistens like coral in all of the neighboring gardens,                5
    And today we have naming of parts.

This is the lower sling swivel. And this
Is the upper sling swivel, whose use you will see,
When you are given your slings. And this is the piling swivel,
Which in your case you have not got. The branches              10
Hold in the gardens their silent, eloquent gestures,
    Which in our case we have not got.

This is the safety-catch, which is always released
With an easy flick of the thumb. And please do not let me
See anyone using his finger. You can do it quite easy          15
If you have any strength in your thumb. The blossoms
Are fragile and motionless, never letting anyone see
    Any of them using their finger.

And this you can see is the bolt. The purpose of this
Is to open the breech, as you see. We can slide it              20
Rapidly backwards and forwards: we call this
Easing the spring. And rapidly backwards and forwards
The early bees are assaulting and fumbling the flowers:
    They call it easing the Spring.

They call it easing the Spring: it is perfectly easy            25
If you have any strength in your thumb: like the bolt,
And the breech, and the cocking-piece, and the point of balance,
Which in our case we have not got; and the almond-blossom
Silent in all of the gardens and the bees going backwards and
    forwards,
    For today we have naming of parts.                          30

HENRY REED (b. 1914)


## Questions

1. Who might be the speaker of the first part of each stanza? Who might be the speaker of the second part of each? What might the situation be?
2. What contrast occurs in each stanza? What words of the first speaker set off the words or thoughts of the second speaker?

3. What differing meanings (or connotations) do these words have?
4. What is the purpose of repeating the phrase "naming of parts"?

## CAN. HIST.

Once upon a colony
there was a land that was
almost a real
country called Canada

But people began to                              5
feel
different
and no longer *Acadien*
or French
and rational                                    10
but *Canadien*
and *Mensch*
and passional

Also no longer English
but Canad*ian*                                  15
and national
(though some were less specific-
ally Canadian
Pacific)
After that it was fashionable                   20
for a time to be Internationable

But now we are all quite
grown up & fir-
mly agreed to assert our right
not to be Amer-                                 25
icans   perhaps
though on the other hand
not ever to be
unamerican
(except for the French                         30
who still want to be *Mensch*)

EARLE BIRNEY (b. 1904)

## Notes

*Mensch* (l.12): a Yiddish word meaning a person, used in contexts such as
"He's a real *mensch*" (he's a decent human being).

Questions
1. What kinds of stories usually begin with the words used at the beginning of the poem? How do these connotations affect your reading of the poem?
2. The poem relies on the connotations of words such as Acadien, French, Canadien, Canadian and American. What connotations of each of these words are important for an understanding of the poem?
3. What do you think is the message or theme of the poem? What was the poet's purpose in writing it?

---

**Poems for Further Study**
These poems in Part One are also rich in connotations:
*How Do I Love Thee?* (p. 24)
*Acquainted With the Night* (p. 32)
*Ulysses* (p. 51)
*When I Heard the Learn'd Astronomer* (p. 98)

---

# Figurative Language

Poets use more figurative language° than we do in ordinary speech. Figurative language is simply any change from the normal order, construction or meaning of words. This type of language gives freshness and strength to an expression and can create a pictorial or descriptive effect. Figurative language commonly shows comparisons between two things that we had never before noticed were similar. Four common types of figurative language are simile, metaphor, personification and apostrophe.

SIMILE AND METAPHOR are the most common types of figurative language. In a simile°, the comparison is indicated by connective words such as "like," "as," and "than," or by verbs such as "seems" and "resembles."

In a metaphor°, the connective word is omitted, and one thing is said to be another. Some form of the verb "to be" is usually used in a metaphor.

In an implied metaphor°, neither a connective word nor the verb "to be" is used in the comparison. The reader must be alert to the inferences of the word.

### • Being Aware of Simile
What comparisons are made in the similes below? What additional meanings do the similes add to the words?

a) The poet claims that even if he were a great orator, without charity he would be "as sounding brass, or a tinkling cymbal."
b) The Indian woman abandoned on an island cries, "Like a wild beast, I am left on this island to die."
c) "I wore my hair like a helmet," says the speaker of her appearance at age sixteen.
d) Later in the same poem, the speaker says, "I had begun to shed knowledge like petals/or scales."
e) The poet describes dying soldiers as "These who die as cattle."
f) Recalling walking with the woman he loves, the speaker says the night "was soft as lips upon our skin."

### • Being Aware of Metaphor

What comparisons are made in the metaphors below? What kinds of meanings do the metaphors add to the sense of the words?

a) Our life is a "play of passion."
b) Our birth is but "a sleep and a forgetting."
c) You are the "salt of the earth."
d) "No man is an island."
e) "When you are the anvil, bear—
When you are the hammer, strike."

### • Being Aware of Implied Metaphor

Find the implied metaphors in these quotations. What two things are compared? What meanings are added by the metaphor?

a) "I remembered that youth would fly fast."
b) The soldier's sigh "Runs in blood down palace walls."

PERSONIFICATION AND APOSTROPHE are figures of speech which are closely related to metaphor. In personification°, a thing, animal or abstract term is given human qualities. That is, a poet compares the non-human to the human. In this way, the abstract quality or idea can be made concrete and, thus, more striking in its meaning.

When poets *address* someone or something either invisible or not ordinarily spoken to, they are using what is called apostrophe°.

### • Being Aware of Personification

What comparisons are made in these excerpts? What is the effect of personifying the object or quality?

a) "Life must be hastening away."
b) "The moving finger writes."

c) "Death lays his icy hands on kings."
d) "Charity suffereth long, and is kind."
e) "I hate that drum's discordant sound,
   Parading round, and round, and round."
f) "The deep moans round with many voices."
g) "I have a rendezvous with Death."


• **Being Aware of Apostrophe**
What does a poet gain by using apostrophe in these excerpts?
a) "Little lamb, who made thee?"
b) "Break, break, break,
   On thy cold gray stones, O Sea!"
c) "O Canada, our home and native land."
d) "Death, be not proud."


### DREAM DEFERRED

What happens to a dream deferred?

Does it dry up
like a raisin in the sun?
Or fester like a sore—
And then run?                                    5
Does it stink like rotten meat?
Or crust and sugar over—
like a syrupy sweet?

Maybe it just sags
like a heavy load.                               10

*Or does it explode?*

LANGSTON HUGHES (1902-1967)


### Questions
In this poem, note the connotations suggested by the similes.
1. In what senses could a dream: dry up, fester, stink, crust and sugar over, sag, explode?
2. Do you think the similes in this poem are well-chosen? Give reasons for your opinion.

## ALL THE WORLD'S A STAGE

All the world's a stage,
And all the men and women merely players;
They have their exits and their entrances,
And one man in his time plays many parts,
His acts being seven ages. At first the infant,                    5
Mewling and puking in the nurse's arms.
Then the whining schoolboy, with his satchel
And shining morning face, creeping like snail
Unwillingly to school. And then the lover,
Sighing like furnace, with a woeful ballad                         10
Made to his mistress' eyebrow. Then a soldier,
Full of strange oaths, and bearded like the pard,
Jealous in honor, sudden, and quick in quarrel,
Seeking the bubble reputation
Even in the cannon's mouth. And then the justice,                  15
In fair round belly with good capon lin'd,
With eyes severe and beard of formal cut,
Full of wise saws and modern instances;
And so he plays his part. The sixt age shifts
Into the lean and slipper'd pantaloon,                             20
With spectacles on nose, and pouch on side,
His youthful hose, well sav'd, a world too wide
For his shrunk shank, and his big manly voice,
Turning again toward childish treble, pipes
And whistles in his sound. Last scene of all,                      25
That ends this strange eventful history,
Is second childishness, and mere oblivion,
Sans teeth, sans eyes, sans taste, sans every thing.

WILLIAM SHAKESPEARE (1564-1616)

## Notes

*All the World's a Stage*: this poem is a speech from the play *As You Like It*.

*mewling* (l.6): crying and whining.

*sighing like a furnace* (l.10): sighing as a furnace emits smoke.

*bearded like the pard* (l.12): having long mustaches like the whiskers of a leopard.

*jealous in honor* (l.13): jealously protective of his honor.

*saws* (l.18): sayings, proverbs, clichés.

*sixt* (l.19): sixth.

*pantaloon* (l.20): foolish old man (from a traditional character in comedy of Shakespeare's time).

**Questions**

1. What metaphor is extended throughout the poem?
2. How are the other images and figurative language related to the central metaphor?
3. What is the dominant rhythm° of the poem? This form is called blank verse°.


## COOK'S MOUNTAINS

By naming them he made them.
They were there
before he came
but they were not the same.
It was his gaze      5
that glazed each one.
He saw
the Glass House Mountains in his glass.
They shone.

And still they shine.
We saw them as we drove—      10
sudden, surrealist, conical
they rose
out of the rain forest.
The driver said,      15
"Those are the Glass House Mountains up ahead."

And instantly they altered to become
the sum of shape and name.
Two strangenesses united into one
more strange than either.      20
Neither of us now
remembers how they looked before they broke
the light to fragments as the driver spoke.

Like mounds of mica,
hive-shaped hothouses,      25
mountains of mirror glimmering
they form
in diamond panes behind the tree ferns of
the dark imagination,
burn and shake      30
the lovely light of Queensland like a bell

reflecting Cook upon a deck
his tongue
silvered with paradox and metaphor.

P.K. PAGE (b. 1916)

## Notes

*Cook's Mountains*: after Captain James Cook (1728-1799), a British explorer and navigator who explored the northeast coast of Australia in 1770.

*surrealist* (l.12): a style in art that tries to portray the workings of the subconscious (as in dreams) by distorting real objects or combining them in unusual ways (see, for example, the works of Salvador Dali).

*mica* (l.24): name given to a group of minerals composed of silicate of aluminum. Occurs in glittering scales in granite.

*Queensland* (l.31): a state in northeastern Australia.

## Questions

1. In what sense is the first line true?
2. How did the name "Glass House Mountains" affect the speaker's view of them?
3. What similes and metaphors occur in the last stanza? For what effects has the poet used them?
4. In what way was Cook's tongue "silvered with paradox and metaphor"?

## THE DESTRUCTION OF SENNACHERIB

The Assyrian came down like the wolf on the fold,
And his cohorts were gleaming in purple and gold;
And the sheen of their spears was like stars on the sea,
When the blue wave rolls nightly on deep Galilee.

Like the leaves of the forest when Summer is green,        5
That host with their banners at sunset were seen:
Like the leaves of the forest when Autumn hath blown,
That host on the morrow lay withered and strown.

For the Angel of Death spread his wings on the blast,
And breathed in the face of the foe as he passed;        10
And the eyes of the sleepers waxed deadly and chill,
And their hearts but once heaved, and forever grew still!

And there lay the steed with his nostril all wide,
But through it there rolled not the breath of his pride;

And the foam of his gasping lay white on the turf,                    15
And cold as the spray of the rock-beating surf.

And there lay the rider distorted and pale,
With the dew on his brow, and the rust on his mail:
And the tents were all silent—the banners alone—
The lances unlifted—the trumpet unblown.                              20

And the widows of Ashur are loud in their wail,
And the idols are broke in the temple of Baal;
And the might of the Gentile, unsmote by the sword,
Hath melted like snow in the glance of the Lord!

GEORGE GORDON, LORD BYRON (1788-1824)

## Notes

*Sennacherib*: a king of Assyria who invaded Palestine in the seventh
century B.C. The story is from the Bible.
*strown* (l.8): strewn, spread about.
*Ashur* (l.21): Assyrian god of War; here meaning the war-dead.
*Baal* (l.22): Caananite god of War. Also god of the Universe and the
source of life and fertility.

## Questions

1. How was the Assyrian army defeated?
2. What contrasting images are there in the poem?
3. What is the dominant rhythm of the poem? Where and why do
variations in the rhythm occur?
Note: This is the poem referred to in the following Ogden Nash poem,
*Very Like a Whale*.

## VERY LIKE A WHALE

One thing that literature would be greatly the better for
Would be a more restricted employment by authors of
   simile and metaphor.
Authors of all races, be they Greeks, Romans, Teutons or
   Celts,
Can't seem just to say that anything is the thing it is but
   have to go out of their way to say that it is like
   something else.
What does it mean when we are told                                    5
That the Assyrian came down like a wolf on the fold?
In the first place, George Gordon Byron had had enough
   experience

To know that it probably wasn't just one Assyrian, it was a
lot of Assyrians.
However, as too many arguments are apt to induce
apoplexy and thus hinder longevity,
We'll let it pass as one Assyrian for the sake of brevity.    10
Now then, this particular Assyrian, the one whose cohorts
were gleaming in purple and gold,
Just what does the poet mean when he says he came down
like a wolf on the fold?
In heaven and earth more than is dreamed of in our
philosophy there are a great many things,
But I don't imagine that among them there is a wolf with
purple and gold cohorts or purple and gold anythings.
No, no, Lord Byron, before I'll believe that this Assyrian was
actually like a wolf I must have some kind of proof;    15
Did he run on all fours and did he have a hairy tail and a
big red mouth and big white teeth and did he say Woof
woof woof?
Frankly I think it very unlikely, and all you were entitled to
say, at the very most,
Was that the Assyrian cohorts came down like a lot of
Assyrian cohorts about to destroy the Hebrew host.
But that wasn't fancy enough for Lord Byron, oh dear me
no, he had to invent a lot of figures of speech and then
interpolate them,
With the result that whenever you mention Old Testament
soldiers to people they say Oh yes, they're the ones that a
lot of wolves dressed up in gold and purple ate them.    20
That's the kind of thing that's being done all the time by
poets, from Homer to Tennyson;
They're always comparing ladies to lilies and veal to
venison.
How about the man who wrote,
Her little feet stole in and out like mice beneath her
petticoat?
Wouldn't anybody but a poet think twice    25
Before stating that his girl's feet were mice?
Then they always say things like that after a winter storm
The snow is a white blanket. Oh it is, is it, all right then,
you sleep under a six-inch blanket of snow and I'll sleep
under a half-inch blanket of unpoetical blanket material
and we'll see which one keeps warm,
And after that maybe you'll begin to comprehend dimly
What I mean by too much metaphor and simile.    30

OGDEN NASH (1902-1971)

**Notes**

*Assyrian* (1.6): refers to Byron's *The Destruction of Sennacherib.*

*apoplexy* (1.9): a disease which numbs the senses and makes movement impossible.

*interpolate* (1.19): insert.

**Questions**

1. What argument does the speaker have with poets who use figurative language?
2. Is the intention of this poem humorous or serious? Give reasons for your opinion.

---

**Poems for Further Study**

The following poems in Part One are rich in figurative language:

*My Brother Dying* (p. 13)

*Death, Be Not Proud* (p. 13)

*L'Envoi: In Beechwood Cemetery* (p. 16)

*Memory* (p. 26)

*She's Like the Swallow* (p. 36)

*I Hate That Drum's Discordant Sound* (p. 46)

*Anthem For Doomed Youth* (p. 47)

*I Have a Rendezvous With Death* (p. 49)

*Song* (p. 54)

*Unemployment (p. 112)*

---

# Irony

Expressions that are rich and full in meaning sometimes distort the words they use, often to the point where the opposite meaning is conveyed. This figure of speech is called irony°. Whenever poets use irony, they always give clues to the reader as to the true meaning of their words.

We also use irony in everyday speech. If someone comes into the house dripping wet, hair in strings and water dribbling from nose and eyebrows, and we say, "You look a little damp," we are using understatement°, one kind of irony. If the person replies, "It's a deluge. I just saw an old guy building an ark," the person is using overstatement°, another kind of irony. The words mean less than what they mean literally.

• Being Aware of Irony

Which of these excerpts are examples of overstatement and which are of understatement? What seems to be the poet's purpose in using each type of irony?

a) "And I will make thee beds of roses,
   And a thousand fragrant posies."
b) "I am one acquainted with the night."
c) "When there was peace, he was for peace; when there was war,
   he went."
d) "A gown made of the finest wool
   With buckles of purest gold."
e) "I love thee to the depth and breadth and height
   My soul can reach."
f) "But I've a rendezvous with Death. . . .
   I shall not fail that rendezvous."

---

Poems to Study

These poems in Part One contain good examples of irony, overstatement, and understatement:

# Imagery

One of the purposes in writing a poem is to allow the reader to experience what the poet experienced. Part of this may require the reader to see or hear what the poet saw or heard. But the poet has only words to recreate these situations and, therefore, uses words that present a picture or sound which the reader can relate to the sense, feeling, tone and intention of the poem.

Sight and sound are only two of the senses. The poet may appeal to any of our senses: touch, taste, smell, bodily sensation (e.g. pain), etc. Imagery° is a word or sequence of words that suggest a sensory experience.

An understanding of the imagery in a poem is extremely important because often the interpretation depends on a grasp of the imagery. Some poems have a series of related images (e.g. water, a lark, the sea). Others may have a series of contrasting images (e.g. brightness and darkness, water and desert, birth and death). The feeling, tone and intention of a poem often emerge through the imagery.

When interpreting imagery, it is best to consider the poem as a whole, to think about all of the poem's images taken together. Relate the imagery to the sense of the poem to find deeper meanings.

• **Being Aware of Imagery**

Find the images in the excerpts below. What senses are appealed to in each? What purposes do the images serve?

a) "For while the tired waves, vainly breaking,
   Seem here no painful inch to gain,
   Far back, through creeks and inlets making,
   Comes silent flooding in, the main."

b) "When Spring comes back with rustling shade
   And apple-blossoms fill the air."

c) "The sea is calm tonight.
   The tide is full, the moon lies fair
   Upon the straits. . . ."
   "Listen! you hear the grating roar
   Of pebbles which the waves draw back, and fling"

d) "And mark in every face I meet
   Marks of weakness, marks of woe"

e) "Far above us where a jay
   Screams his matins to the day,
   Capped with gold and amethyst,
   Like a vapour from the forge
   Of a giant somewhere hid."

## EROSION

It took the sea a thousand years,
A thousand years to trace
The granite features of this cliff,
In crag and scarp and base.

It took the sea an hour one night,                    5
An hour of storm to place
The sculpture of these granite seams
Upon a woman's face.

E.J. PRATT (1882-1964)


## Questions

1. What two contrasting images does the poem present?
2. How does the poem show a relationship between these two images?
3. What two different meanings does the word "granite" have in the poem?
4. Note the rhyme° at the end of lines 2, 4, 6 and 8. How does this give unity° to the poem?
5. Who might the speaker of these words be? What might the situation be in which they are spoken?


## THE EVE OF ST. AGNES
*—an excerpt*

St. Agnes' Eve—Ah, bitter chill it was!
The owl, for all his feathers, was a-cold;
The hare limped trembling through the frozen grass,
And silent was the flock in woolly fold:
Numb were the Beadsman's fingers, while he told          5
His rosary, and while his frosted breath,
Like pious incense from a censer old,
Seemed taking flight for heaven, without a death,
Past the sweet Virgin's picture, while his prayer he saith.

His prayer, he saith, this patient, holy man;            10
Then takes his lamp, and riseth from his knees,
And back returneth, meager, barefoot, wan,
Along the chapel aisle by slow degrees:
The sculptured dead, on each side, seem to freeze,
Emprisoned in black, purgatorial rails:                 15
Knights, ladies, praying in dumb orat'ries,
He passeth by; and his weak spirit fails
To think how they may ache in icy hoods and mails.

Northward he turneth through a little door,
And scarce three steps, ere Music's golden tongue          20
Flattered to tears this aged man and poor;
But no—already had his death-bell rung:
The joys of all his life were said and sung:
His was harsh penance on St. Agnes' Eve:
Another way he went, and soon among          25
Rough ashes sat he for his soul's reprieve,
And all night kept awake, for sinners' sake to grieve.

JOHN KEATS (1795-1821)

## Notes

*The eve of St. Agnes*: the night of this feast day, Jan. 20th, is said in folklore to be the coldest night of the year.

*Beadsman* (1.5): a pensioner bound to pray for the souls of his benefactors.

*rosary* (1.6): a set of 165 prayers, with many repetitions of the same prayer, to the mother of God. The prayers are counted on a string of beads called a rosary.

*censer* (1.7): container for incense.

*Virgin* (1.9): the Blessed Virgin Mary, the mother of Jesus.

*purgatorial* (1.15): like purgatory, a place where souls are sent after death to be purified before they enter heaven, according to Catholic tradition.

*orat'ries* (1.16): oratories; small chapels, places of prayer containing statues.

## Questions

1. These are the first three stanzas of a longer poem. These stanzas have been called "the coldest" in the English language. What images create the sensations of intense cold and chill?

## THE IMMIGRANTS

They are allowed to inherit
the sidewalks involved as palmlines, bricks
exhausted and soft, the deep
lawnsmells, orchards whorled
to the land's contours, the inflected weather          5

only to be told they are too poor
to keep it up, or someone

has noticed and wants to kill them; or the towns
pass laws which declare them obsolete.

I see them coming                                      10
up from the hold smelling of vomit,
infested, emaciated, their skins grey
with travel; as they step on shore

the old countries recede, become
perfect, thumbnail castles preserved                   15
like gallstones in a glass bottle, the
towns dwindle upon the hillsides
in a light paperweight-clear.

They carry their carpetbags and trunks
with clothes, dishes, the family pictures;             20
they think they will make an order
like the old one, sow miniature orchards,
carve children and flocks out of wood

but always they are too poor, the sky
is flat, the green fruit shrivels                       25
in the prairie sun, wood is for burning;
and if they go back, the towns

in time have crumbled, their tongues
stumble among awkward teeth, their ears
are filled with the sound of breaking glass.           30
I wish I could forget them
and so forget myself:

my mind is a wide pink map
across which move year after year
arrows and dotted lines, further and further,          35
people in railway cars

their heads stuck out of the windows
at stations, drinking milk or singing,
their features hidden with beards or shawls
day and night riding across an ocean of unknown        40
land to an unknown land.

MARGARET ATWOOD (b. 1939)


## Notes

*whorled* (l.4): curled or coiled.

*gallstones* (l.16): small, hard crystalized pieces of bile from the liver which are more likely to form in the gall bladders of older or obese individuals. They can cause pain and inflammation.

## Questions

1. What is the theme° of this poem?
2. What images are especially striking in developing or illustrating the theme?
3. What senses are stimulated by these images?


### THE SHARK

He seemed to know the harbour,
So leisurely he swam;
His fin,
Like a piece of sheet-iron,
Three-cornered                                                    5
And with knife-edge,
Stirred not a bubble
As it moved
With its base-line on the water.

His body was tubular                                              10
And tapered
And smoke-blue,
And as he passed the wharf
He turned,
And snapped at a flat-fish                                       15
That was dead and floating.
And I saw the flash of a white throat,
And a double row of white teeth,
And eyes of metallic grey,
Hard and narrow and slit.                                        20

Then out of the harbour,
With that three-cornered fin
Shearing without a bubble the water
Lithely,
Leisurely,                                                       25
He swam—
That strange fish,
Tubular, tapered, smoke-blue,
Part vulture, part wolf,
Part neither—for his blood was cold.                             30

E.J. PRATT (1882-1964)

**Questions**
1. What feelings about the shark does the poem stimulate?
2. What images (words or expressions) create those feelings?

---

**Poems for Further Study**
Almost any poem could be used to explore imagery, but these poems in Part One contain especially effective images:
*Chronology* (p. 4)
*The Forsaken* (p. 33)
*Wabanaki Song* (p. 35)
*The Lonely Land* (p. 37)
*Psalm 23* (p. 54)
*To Autumn* (p. 87)

---

# Symbol and Allusion

Certain objects stand for more than what they are. A flag is more than a colored piece of cloth. A fat, white-bearded man in a red suit is more than just that. The flag represents all our feelings about a country. The jolly fat man represents the meaning of Christmas. Such objects are symbols°. Symbols are useful for poets because they are rich in connotation.

Allusions° are closely related to symbols. An allusion is a word or phrase that refers to something or someone in history or in literature. Through the use of allusion, the tales which surround well-known individuals or events are made part of our understanding of the present. To say that a man is old and has suffered much, but has also achieved much, is a fine sentiment. To say he is, or is like, Ulysses states much more for those who know of the celebrated wanderings of the Greek hero.

### • Being Aware of Symbols
What symbols are used in these excerpts? What do they symbolize? What meanings do the symbols add to the poems?

   a)                           "Round the decay
        Of that colossal wreck, boundless and bare
        The lone and level sands stretch far away."

b) "Does he picture us buzzards
   Circling round his bed?"
c) "One luminary clock against the sky
   Proclaimed the time was neither wrong nor right."

• **Being Aware of Allusion**
What allusions are made in these excerpts? Use a dictionary or other reference book if you are unfamiliar with the person or thing alluded to. What meanings do the allusions add to the poem?

a) "Sophocles long ago
   Heard it on the Aegean"
b) "Then chase itself down the hill
   And neigh like Boanerges"
c) "An angel writing in a book of gold"
d) "Into the valley of Death
   Rode the six hundred."

### THE HOURGLASS

Do but consider this small dust,
   Here running in the glass,
     By atoms moved;
Could you believe that this,
   The body ever was                5
     Of one that loved?
And in his mistress' flame, playing like a fly,
   Turned to cinders by her eye?
   Yes; and in death, as life, unblest,
     To have't expressed,             10
   Even ashes of lovers find no rest.

BEN JONSON (1572-1637)

**Note**
*fly* (l.7): any two-winged insect including the moth and the butterfly.

**Question**
1. What does the hourglass symbolize for the speaker?

> **Poems for Further Study**
> These poems in Part One contain interesting symbols and/or allusions:

# Figurative Language and Its Uses

Because there are no firm divisions among the various figures of speech, you may find any given example classified as more than one type of figurative language. The important thing is not that you label each one exactly, but that you recognize them and understand how poets use them to achieve a specific purpose.

Figurative language serves two closely related purposes:
- to engage the emotions and imagination of the reader;
- to elicit an immediate and strong response from the reader.

The various kinds of figurative language, irony, imagery, symbol and allusion suggest emotional overtones which deepen the meanings of the words on the page. To the intellectual concept of the word, the poet adds emotion. The emotion creates a feeling° and a tone° which help to clarify the poet's intention° in the poem.

We respond more quickly and more emotionally to a concrete object than we do to an abstract idea. If we hear the word "love", we respond with a generalized intellectual concept. If we hear the name of a person we love, we respond in a more direct and emotional way. So figurative language helps the poet to make abstract ideas concrete.

To be appreciated by the reader, figurative language must relate to the reader's experience. A continuing problem for modern readers when we read poems from the past is that we may not understand the symbols, allusions and imagery the poet uses. The good reader keeps a dictionary at hand and makes frequent use of encyclopedia and reference books on matters such as Greek mythology and the Bible.

# Poems For Interpretation

Read the following poems several times to deepen your interpretations. Especially note the poets' uses of figurative language. Create your own questions for study and discussion.

## THE UNNAMED LAKE

It sleeps among the thousand hills
    Where no man ever trod,
And only nature's music fills
    The silences of God.

Great mountains tower above its shore,         5
    Green rushes fringe its brim,
And o'er its breast for evermore
    The wanton breezes skim.

Dark clouds that intercept the sun
    Go there in Spring to weep,         10
And there, when Autumn days are done,
    White mists lie down to sleep.

Sunrise and sunset crown with gold
    The peaks of ageless stone,
Where winds have thundered from of old     15
    And storms have set their throne.

No echoes of the world afar
    Disturb it night or day,
But sun and shadow, moon and star
    Pass and repass for aye.         20

'Twas in the grey of early dawn,
    When first the lake we spied,
And fragments of a cloud were drawn
    Half down the mountain side.

Along the shore a heron flew,         25
    And from a speck on high,
That hovered in the deepening blue,
    We heard the fish-hawk's cry.

Among the cloud-capt solitudes,
    No sound the silence broke,         30
Save when, in whispers down the woods,
    The guardian mountains spoke.

Through tangled brush and dewy brake,
  Returning whence we came,
We passed in silence, and the lake                    35
  We left without a name.

FREDERICK GEORGE SCOTT (1861-1944)


### this is a poem

this is a poem for my father's gravestone
a grave poem for my father's stone
a father for my poem's gravestone
a groan for my father's grave

father   i will bless your grave with poems
i will stone your grave with blessings father
i will father my poems with your blessings
i will bless my poems with your fathering
father i will

father your blessings on my grave poem
father on my poem's grave
bless      my poem      my father's grave
bless the stones my father gave

                my stones bless my father's poem

                        father
                    on my poems
                    your blessing

PAUL DUTTON (b. 1943)


### BUTTERFLY ON ROCK

The large yellow wings, black-fringed,
were motionless

They say the soul of a dead person
will settle like that on the still face

But I thought: the rock has borne this;          5
this butterfly is the rock's grace,
its most obstinate and secret desire
to be a thing alive made manifest

Forgot were the two shattered porcupines
I had seen die in the bleak forest.              10

Pain is unreal; death, an illusion:
There is no death in all the land,
I heard my voice cry;
And brought my hand down on the butterfly
And felt the rock move beneath my hand.                    15

IRVING LAYTON (b. 1912)


## THE BEAR ON THE DELHI ROAD

Unreal     tall as a myth
by the road the Himalayan bear
is beating the brilliant air
with his crooked arms
About him two men     bare                    5
spindly as locusts     leap

One pulls on a ring
in the great soft nose     His mate
flicks     flicks with a stick
up at the rolling eyes                    10

They have not led him here
down from the fabulous hills
to this bald alien plain
and the clamorous world     to kill
but simply to teach him to dance                    15

They are peaceful both     these spare
men of Kashmir     and the bear
alive is their living     too
If     far on the Delhi way
around him galvanic they dance                    20
it is merely to wear     wear
from his shaggy body the tranced
wish forever to stay
only an ambling bear
four-footed in berries                    25

It is no more joyous for them
in this hot dust to prance
out of reach of the praying claws
sharpened to paw for ants
in the shadows of deodars                    30
It is not easy to free
myth from reality

or rear this fellow up
to lurch    lurch with them
in the tranced dancing of men                                    35

EARLE BIRNEY (b. 1904)


**Notes**

*galvanic* (1.20): producing a current of electricity; sudden, startling.
*deodars* (1.30): cedars which grow in the Himalayas.


## THE LISTENERS

"Is there anybody there?" said the Traveller,
    Knocking on the moonlit door;
And his horse in the silence champed the grasses
    Of the forest's ferny floor;
And a bird flew up out of the turret,                            5
    Above the Traveller's head;
And he smote upon the door again a second time;
    "Is there anybody there?" he said.
But no one descended to the Traveller;
    No head from the leaf-fringed sill                           10
Leaned over and looked into his grey eyes,
    Where he stood perplexed and still.
But only a host of phantom listeners
    That dwelt in the lone house then
Stood listening in the quiet of the moonlight                    15
    To that voice from the world of men:
Stood thronging the faint moonbeams on the dark stair,
    That goes down to the empty hall,
Hearkening in an air stirred and shaken
    By the lonely Traveller's call.                              20
And he felt in his heart their strangeness,
    Their stillness answering his cry,
While his horse moved, cropping the dark turf,
    'Neath the starred and leafy sky;
For he suddenly smote on the door, even                          25
    Louder, and lifted his head:
"Tell them I came, and no one answered,
    That I kept my word," he said.
Never the least stir made the listeners,
    Though every word he spake                                   30
Fell echoing through the shadowiness of the still house
    From the one man left awake:

Ay, they heard his foot upon the stirrup,
 And the sound of iron on stone,
And how the silence surged softly backward,     35
 When the plunging hoofs were gone.

WALTER de la MARE (1873-1956)


**Note**

*champed* (l.3): bit and chewed, with connotations of impatience.


## WALTER DE LA MARE TELLS THE LISTENER ABOUT JACK AND JILL

Up to the top of the haunted turf
 They climbed on the moonlit hill.
Not a leaf rustled in the underbrush;
 The listening air was still,

And only the noise of the water pail     5
 As it struck on a jutting stone,
Clattered and jarred against the silence
 As the two trod on alone.

Up to the moonlit peak they went;
 And, though not a word would they say,     10
Their thoughts outnumbered a poet's love-songs
 In the first green weeks of May.

The stealthy shadows crept closer;
 They clutched at the hem of Jill's gown;
And there at the very top she stumbled,     15
 And Jack came shuddering down.

Their cries rang out against the stillness,
 Pitiful and high and thin.
And the echoes edged back still further
 As the silence gathered them in.     20

LOUIS UNTERMEYER (1885-1977)

# 2 HOW POEMS ARE SHAPED

## Introduction

The most obvious organization of poems is according to sentences and stanzas°. Sentences in poetry perform the same functions as they do in prose. In general, a sentence is a statement about something. Stanzas in poetry may be compared to paragraphs in prose, but while a paragraph in prose is usually a group of sentences, a stanza in poetry may be one or more sentences or may be only a part of a sentence.

When reading a poem, especially for the first time, note the punctuation that indicates sentence parts and sentence types (statements, questions, exclamations, commands); and note the divisions the poet makes between the parts of the poem by placing certain ideas in certain stanzas. We will give a more detailed description of stanzas later in this chapter.

Poems are also organized according to rhythm° and often rhyme°, though not all poems contain rhyme. Think of stanzas and sentences as the large scale organizers in a poem while rhythm and rhyme operate on the small scale within words and lines or groups of lines.

Rhythm has been called the dance or movement of poetry while sound is the song. Poetry contains movements and sounds which themselves convey meanings and add to the meanings of the words in the poem. In this chapter, we shall concentrate on the contribution of rhythm and sound to poetry.

# Rhythm

We usually associate rhythm with music and poetry, but there is rhythm in everyday language too. If you read this sentence aloud, you will notice that some words or parts of words are stressed more than others, and there are pauses of varying lengths between groups of words. These stresses and pauses are the basis for rhythm, but in everyday speech they are usually not organized into any regular pattern. It is the pattern that creates rhythm in poetry.

To create a pattern, poets must select words that are appropriate to the full meaning they want to convey and which also allow for stress in the appropriate places. Poets may also change the order of words. For example, in everyday speech we might say:

I am standing beside my dark house on this long, dull street again.

A poet might say:

Dark house, by which once more I stand

Here in the long unlovely street. . . .

What additional meanings does the poet gain by changing the order of words and by using rhythm?

This regular pattern of stressed and unstressed syllables is called metre.° Metre is all around us in songs, dances, in dripping taps and in the absent-minded finger tapping we do when we are nervous or bored.

Rhythm, then, is created by a pattern of stressed and unstressed syllables in words and by the pauses between words. The rhythm itself can convey meaning. You yourself use emphasis and pauses to add meaning to the sense of the words you speak.

## • Being Aware of Emphasis

Say the sentence below in different ways to convey the meanings listed below it:

"Patti, please close the door."

a) Several people are present, and Patti is selected.

b) Patti has just opened the door.

c) Patti has just closed the window.

d) Patti has been asked several times, and now the speaker is being sarcastically polite.

e) The speaker is coaxing Patti.

f) The speaker is ordering Patti.

What other kinds of meanings can you convey using the same words but changing the emphasis and pauses?

That is one use of rhythm—to convey meanings beyond the sense° of the words. These additional meanings contribute to the feeling° and tone° of the poem and help to make the poet's intention° clear.

Rhythm and rhyme have other uses too. For example, a reliable bit of folk wisdom about the weather is that if the sky has a reddish color in the evening, there will be good weather the next day. But if there is a reddish color in the morning, the weather will be bad that day. Most people have trouble remembering which foretells good weather and which predicts bad, unless they remember the rhythmic,

"Red sky at night sailor's delight;
Red sky at morning sailor take warning."

What other verses do you know that help you remember certain facts?

Another use of rhyme and rhythm is suggested by epitaphs—sayings on tombstones. For example,

"Life is a jest; and all things show it.
I thought so once, but now I know it."

Or,

"Beneath this stone, a lump of clay,
Lies Uncle Peter Dan'ls,
Who early in the month of May
Took off his winter flannels."

Why are these final statements to a person's life often written in verse? Humor aside, rhythm and rhyme can give the words an air of permanence and importance. As Shakespeare states,

"Not marble, nor the gilded monuments
Of princes, shall outlive this pow'rful rhyme."

So when writing about important events or expressing ideas of importance, poets often use rhythm (or metre) and rhyme. The regular, deliberate patterns show that the language is at a level above the ordinary as befits the content of the poem. You should note, however, that many modern poems do not contain rhyme and may be quite irregular in rhythm. The reason for this is that modern poets often try new forms of expression to give their poems freshness and strength.

When reading a poem, it is important to note the rhythm because it is often a clue to its sense, feeling, tone and intention. Usually, the words are arranged so that the rhythm occurs naturally as we read. When reading aloud, let the words carry the meaning. Do not overstress the rhythm; but be aware of it, and read in a natural manner, trusting the poet to show where the rhythm occurs and why.

## TODAY IN HISTORY

*August 22, 1903*
*Expedition of the Neptune under Commander Low*
*to Hudson Straits*

While we welter
In the swelter
Of the pestilential Heat
Drinking Sodas
In Pagodas       5
At the corner of the Street
   It seems to me
   That it would be
   My highest aspiration
   To sail away       10
   On a Holiday
   Or Arctic Exploration.
Let me lie in my Pyjamas on the ice of Baffin's Bay,
In the thinnest of chemises where the Polar breezes play,
Underneath a frozen awning let me lie at ease a span,    15
While beneath the bright Aurora roars the ventilation fan.

Can you wonder now that Nansen and that Peary, and that
   Low,
Should wander forth,
And struggle North,
As far as they can go?       20
When the hero
Under zero
Lives on frozen lager beer,
And a demi-can
Of Pemmican       25
You need not shed a tear.
He seeks a higher latitude,
I quite admit the feat;
The reason is a platitude
He's crazy with the heat.       30

STEPHEN LEACOCK (1869-1944)


## Notes
*chemises* (l.14): undergarments.
*Aurora* (l.16): aurora borealis or northern lights; a natural phenomenon
   in the sky consisting of patches, rays, streamers and arcs of light in
   shades of violet, blue, green, yellow and red.

*Pemmican* (l.25): a long-lasting meat paste.
*platitude* (l.29): dull, commonplace remark.

Questions

1. What reasons does the speaker give for explorations of the North?
2. What does the rhythm add to the humor?
3. Read the poem aloud, letting the words illustrate the rhythm. The poem also lends itself well to choral or group reading, perhaps with alternating parts.

## HOW THE HELPMATE
## OF BLUE-BEARD
## MADE FREE WITH A DOOR

A maiden from the Bosphorus, with eyes as bright as phosphorus,
Once wed the wealthy bailiff of the Caliph of Kelat.
Though diligent and zealous, he became a slave to jealousy;
Considering her beauty 'twas his duty to be that.
When business would necessitate a journey he would hestitate,                                                              5
But, fearing to disgust her, he would trust her with his keys,
Remarking to her prayerfully, "I beg you'll use them carefully.
Don't look what I deposit in that closet, if you please."
It might be mentioned casually, that blue as lapis-lazuli
He dyed his hair, his lashes, his mustaches and his beard,   10
And, just because he did it, he aroused his wife's timidity;
Her terror she dissembled, but she trembled when he neared.
This feeling insalubrious soon made her most lugubrious,
And bitterly she missed her elder sister Marie Anne:
She asked if she might write her to come down and spend
a night or two;                                                               15
Her husband answered rightly and politely: "Yes, you can."
Blue-Beard, the Monday following, his jealous feelings swallowing,
Packed all his clothes together in a leather-bound valise,
Then, feigning reprehensibly, he started out ostensibly
By traveling to learn a bit of Smyrna and of Greece.         20
His wife made but a cursory inspection of the nursery,
The kitchen and the airy little dairy were a bore,
As well as big or scanty rooms, and billiard, bath,
and anterooms,
But not that interdicted and restricted little door.

For, all her curiosity awakened by the closet he          25
So carefully had hidden and forbidden her to see,
This damsel disobedient did something inexpedient
And in the key-hole tiny turned the shiny little key.
Then started back impulsively, and shrieked aloud
    convulsively;
Three heads of maids he'd wedded—and beheaded—
    met her eye.          30
And turning round much terrified, her darkest fears
    were verified,
For Blue-Beard stood behind her, come to find her on the
    sly.
Perceiving she was fated to be soon decapitated, too,
She telegraphed her brothers and some others what
    she feared.
And Sister Anne looked out for them in readiness to shout
    for them          35
Whenever in the distance with assistance they appeared.
But only from her battlement she saw some dust that
    cattle meant.
The ordinary story isn't glory, but a jest.
But here's the truth unqualified: the husband wasn't
    mollified;
Her head is in his bloody little study with the rest!

The Moral: Wives, we must allow, who to their husbands
    will not bow,
A stern and dreadful lesson learn when, as you've read,
    they're cut in turn.

GUY WETMORE CARRYL (1873-1904)


## Notes

*Bosphorous* (l:1): Bosporous (now the Dardanelles) Strait separating
    Europe from Asian Turkey.
*lapis-lazuli* (l.9): a bright-blue gemstone.
*insalubrious* (l.13): unhealthy.
*lugubrious* (l.13): mournful, sorrowful.
*interdicted* (l.24): forbidden.
*mollified* (l.39): appeased, softened in temper.


## Questions

1. What is the rather gruesome story of this poem? How does the rhythm
    affect our interpretation of the poem?

2. What is the author's tone in the poem? Give reasons for your opinion.
3. Read the poem aloud, perhaps with other students, to appreciate the rhythm.

**PATTERNS OF RHYTHM** are found in a poem by means of the technique called scansion.° In scansion we count the accents and unstressed syllables and divide them into feet.° Note that scansion is a way to find out the "mechanical" techniques the poet used to achieve certain effects. The meaning of the poem always comes first. We use scansion to dig deeper into the poet's craft, to deepen our appreciation of poetry and to learn methods we can apply in writing poetry.

The unit of rhythm is called a foot.° There are five common feet in English poetry. Two of these are based on two syllables:

- the iambic      (e.g. dĕstróy)
- the trochaic    (e.g. wándĕr)

The iambic is by far the most common. Two other feet are based on three syllables:

- the anapestic   (e.g. ĭntĕrvéne)
- the dactylic    (e.g. mérrĭlў)

The fifth common foot has two stressed syllables:

- the spondaic    (e.g. fóotbáll)

You will find many variations on these feet as you read poems, which makes scanning poetry somewhat tricky. Indeed, your scansion may not agree with someone else's. Most poems have one dominant type of rhythm (e.g. iambic), but there will be other feet used occasionally as well. A poem that never varied would become very dull. As you read note the effects certain rhythms have. Note also the variations in the pattern. You may find in some lines unstressed syllables that do not seem to fit the pattern. These are called slack syllables.° Often the poet varies the rhythm to emphasize important words and ideas.

When you scan whole lines of poetry, you will want to state the number of feet in each line. The terms for counting are from the Latin words:

| | | | |
|---|---|---|---|
| mono | —one | penta | —five |
| di | —two | hexa | —six |
| tri | —three | hepta | —seven |
| tetra | —four | octa | —eight. |

To each of these is added the word metre, giving us:

| | | |
|---|---|---|
| monometre —one foot | pentametre —five feet |
| dimetre  —two feet | hexametre  —six feet |
| trimetre  —three feet | heptametre —seven feet |
| tetrametre —four feet | octametre  —eight feet. |

Now we are ready to describe the rhythm of a line of poetry. If, for example, the line is iambic and has five feet, it is called iambic pentametre:
"Not marble, nor the gilded monuments"
Here is another common rhythm:
"Like a child from the womb, like a ghost from the tomb."
Describe the rhythm of that line.

THE EFFECTS OF RHYTHM are most clearly seen in the emotional meanings conveyed in a poem. For example, feelings of sadness or joy are often partly the result of the flow or movement of the words in a poem.

Iambic° ($u/$) is the most common English foot, perhaps because there is a tendency in English for words to be accented on the second syllable and because many function words have one syllable and the more substantive words which follow them are stressed (e.g. the dog has run to school). Therefore iambic rhythm seems most natural and most like ordinary speech. The trochaic° ($/u$) rhythm reverses the natural flow and makes a line seem to move more roughly. The anapestic° foot ($uu/$) with the two light beats before the accent gives a leaping motion often used in humorous verse or in descriptions of swift action. The dactylic° ($//u$) begins with an accent and therefore often gives a thrusting, driving movement.

The poet varies the motion in a poem by changing the metre at times or by using more accented one-syllable words. In general, many unaccented syllables quicken the pace, while many accented syllables slow it.

Read and discuss the poems that follow. To deepen your appreciation, note how poets use rhythm, and note the effects they gain by using certain kinds of rhythm and by varying the regular pattern.

## SHE WALKS IN BEAUTY

She Walks in Beauty *refers to Lady Wilmot Horton, whom Byron had seen at a ball, attired in mourning with spangles on her dress.*

She walks in beauty, like the night
   Of cloudless climes and starry skies;
And all that's best of dark and bright
   Meet in her aspect and her eyes:
Thus mellowed to that tender light        5
   Which heaven to gaudy day denies.

One shade the more, one ray the less,
    Had half impaired the nameless grace
Which waves in every raven tress,
    Or softly lightens o'er her face;                    10
Where thoughts serenely sweet express
    How pure, how dear their dwelling-place.

And on that cheek, and o'er that brow,
    So soft, so calm, yet eloquent,
The smiles that win, the tints that glow,              15
    But tell of days in goodness spent,
A mind at peace with all below,
    A heart whose love is innocent!

GEORGE GORDON, LORD BYRON (1788-1824)


Notes

*climes* (l.2): regions, especially those demarcated by climate.
*aspect* (l.4): appearance (This word is rich in connotations. Use a dictionary as a guide to some of them).
*eloquent* (l.14): speaking forcefully and gracefully.

## Questions

1. What is the dominant metre in this poem?
2. What variations do you find in the metre? Why do you think the poet has varied the metre at these points?
3. How does the rhythm contribute to the sense, feeling, tone and intention of the poem?


## METRICAL FEET

Trochee trips from long to short;
From long to long in solemn sort
Slow Spondee stalks; strong foot! yet ill able
Ever to come up with Dactyl trisyllable.
Iambics march from short to long—                      5
With a leap and a bound the swift Anapests throng;
One syllable long, with one short at each side,
Amphibrachys hastes with a stately stride—
First and last being long, middle short, Amphimacer
Strikes his thundering hoofs like a proud high-bred Racer. 10
If Derwent be innocent, steady, and wise,
And delight in the things of earth, water, and skies;

Tender warmth at his heart, with these meters to show it,
With sound sense in his brains, may make Derwent a poet—
May crown him with fame, and must win him the love    15
Of his father on earth and his Father above.
      My dear, dear child!
Could you stand upon Skiddaw, you would not from its
   whole ridge
See a man who so loves you as your fond S. T. COLERIDGE.

SAMUEL TAYLOR COLERIDGE (1792-1834)

## Notes

*Amphibrachys* (l.8) and *Aphimacer* (l.9): two types of rhythmic foot,
illustrated in the poem.

*Derwent* (l.11): Coleridge's younger son. The poet originally wrote this
poem for his elder son Hartley but later revised it. Coleridge himself
put the long and short marks over the syllables.

*Skiddaw* (l.18): a mountain in the lake country where Coleridge lived when
he was younger.

---

**Poems For Further Study**

These poems in Part One are good illustrations of the use and effects
of rhythm:

*The Passionate Shepherd To His Love* (p. 25)
*I Hate That Drum's Discordant Sound* (p. 46)
*In Flanders Fields* (p. 48)
*An Autumn Song* (p. 87)
*The Tiger* (p. 89)
*I Like to See It Lap the Miles* (p. 97)
*The Ryans and the Pittmans* (p. 105)

---

# Sound In Poetry

When we think of sound in poetry, we usually think of rhyme, so we will
consider that first. Thereafter we will look at how poets use the sounds of
words.

The uses of rhyme are similar to those of rhythm. Rhyme raises the
level of language above that of ordinary speech and gives the words an air
of importance and permanence. Rhyme is also used as a means of organiz-

ing a poem. When rhyme occurs at the ends of lines, it links the lines together and usually the meanings are somehow connected as well. Rhyme also provides a method of emphasis. Rhyming words are noticeable, and when they occur in important places, they give extra emphasis to those words. When coupled with the stress attained by rhythm, such words can be very important to the total meaning of the poem.

THE KINDS OF RHYME are many and varied. Rhymes are *exact* when the vowel sound and any sounds following it are the same. Note that we must attend to the sounds of the words, not their spellings. Rhymes may be more than one syllable in length. One syllable rhyming words or words that are stressed on the last syllable are called single rhymes° (also "masculine or male"). For example: pail—rail; divorce—remorse. Two-syllable rhyming words or words in which the next to last syllables are stressed are called double rhymes° (also "feminine or female"). For example: gladness—madness; turtle—fertile.

### • Being Aware of Rhyme

What kinds of rhymes occur in these pairs?

   red—bread

   wealthily—stealthily

   cling to her—sing to her

English does not contain as many rhymes as some other languages. In fact, a large number of common English words cannot be rhymed. Can you find rhymes for any of these words?

   circle, desert, orange, month, virtue, wisdom

One type of inexact rhyme is slant rhyme° (also called near rhyme, off rhyme, or partial rhyme). In slant rhyme, the final consonants are the same but the preceding vowel is different. For example, stone—sun, rain—moon.

A note of caution about rhyme: because the pronunciation of words changes with time, some words that once rhymed do not rhyme in modern speech. For example, "tea" once rhymed with "say" and "die" with "me." When reading poems from before the twentieth century, be alert to possible differences in pronunciation because some words that appear not to rhyme may have rhymed when the poet wrote them.

The danger in writing rhyming poetry is that the rhyme can become boring and can actually distract the reader from the sense of the words. Rhyme is effective when it is fresh and unexpected, when it gives emphasis where it is intended and when it weaves the poem together. The best way to see rhyme at work is to examine some poems.

## MIDNIGHT

From where I sit, I see the stars,
   And down the chilly floor
The moon between the frozen bars
   Is glimmering dim and hoar.

Without in many a peakéd mound           5
   The glinting snowdrifts lie;
There is no voice or living sound;
   The embers slowly die.

Yet some wild thing is in mine ear;
   I hold my breath and hark:             10
Out of the depth I seem to hear
   A crying in the dark;

No sound of man or wife or child,
   No sound of beast that groans,
Or of the wind that whistles wild,       15
   Or of the tree that moans:

I know not what it is I hear;
   I bend my head and hark;
I cannot drive it from mine ear,
   That crying in the dark.             20

ARCHIBALD LAMPMAN (1861-1899)

## Notes
*hoar* (l.4): heavy frost.
*hark* (l.10): listen carefully.

## Questions
1. Notice the rhyme scheme° or pattern in this poem. To mark a rhyme
   scheme, do the following:
   - Label the first rhyme at the end of a line as *a*.
   - All words that occur at the ends of lines that rhyme with *a* are also
     labelled *a*.
   - The next rhyming word you find at the end of a line is labelled *b*, and
     all words that rhyme with it at the ends of lines are labelled *b*.
   - Continue this way marking rhymes *c*, *d*, etc.
   For example, the rhyme scheme of the first six lines of *Today in
   History* (p. 153) is *aabccb*. In a long poem, each stanza is marked
   separately. In a shorter poem, the scheme may be spread over the
   whole poem.

2. Which two stanzas in *Midnight* match each other in rhyme? Why do you think the poet has repeated these rhymes?
3. Does the regular rhyme pattern add to or detract from the interest and meaning of the poem? Give reasons for your opinion.

## CLEVER TOM CLINCH GOING TO BE HANGED

As clever Tom Clinch, while the rabble was bawling,
Rode stately through Holborn, to die in his calling;
He stopped at the George for a bottle of sack,
And promised to pay for it when he'd come back.
His waistcoat and stockings, and breeches were white,    5
His cap had a new cherry ribbon to tie 't.
The maids to the doors and the balconies ran,
And said, lack-a-day! he's a proper young man.
But, as from the windows the ladies he spied,
Like a beau in the box, he bowed low on each side;    10
And when his last speech the loud hawkers did cry,
He swore from his cart, it was all a damned lie.

The hangman for pardon fell down on his knee;
Tom gave him a kick in the guts for his fee.
Then said, I must speak to the people a little,    15
But I'll see you all damned before I will *whittle*.
My honest friend Wild, may he long hold his place,
He lengthened my life with a whole year of grace.
Take courage, dear comrades, and be not afraid,
Nor slip this occasion to follow your trade.    20
My conscience is clear, and my spirits are calm,
And thus I go off without Pray'r-Book or Psalm.
Then follow the practice of clever Tom Clinch,
Who hung like a hero, and never would flinch.

JONATHAN SWIFT (1667-1745)

## Notes

*Holborn* (l.2): the road leading to the gallows.
*George* (l.3): a tavern
*a beau in the box* (l.10): a well-dressed gentleman in a theatre box seat
*hawkers did cry* (l.11): the "dying words" of condemned criminals were often written beforehand by hack writers and offered for sale at the hanging.
*whittle* (l.16): confess at the gallows.

*Wild* (l.17): an underworld figure at the time the poem was written (the 1720's).

*follow your trade* (l.20): pickpockets, no doubt active in the crowd at that moment.

## Question

1. How does the rhythm add to the light-hearted tone of the poem?

### RHYMES

Two respectable rhymes
skipped out of their pages
like two proud roosters
from golden cages;

They walked many a mile                                    5
in search of a home,
but could find no space
for themselves in a poem.

They grew tired and sad
but wherever they went                                    10
nobody advertised
poems for rent.

People whispered and said:
haven't you heard
that a rhyming word                                       15
is considered absurd?

In modern times
who needs rhymes?
Those high-flying words
went out with the birds.                                  20

At last one night
all weary and worn
they came to a house
in a field of corn;

and there lived a man                                     25
who still wrote lines
according to rules
from olden times.

So he took them in
with doubles and pairs,                                   30

and set them to music,
and gave them new airs.

Now they ring again
their bells and chimes,
and the children all sing                                    35
those respectable rhymes,

with one rhyme inside
and another one out:
the rhymes were befriended
and my poem is ended.                                        40

Y.Y. SEGAL (1896-1954)
(Translated by Miriam Waddington)

## Questions

1. What value does the speaker see in rhyme?
2. What uses does the poet make of rhyme?
3. The last stanza refers to "one rhyme inside/and another one out,"
   meaning rhyme within lines (internal) and rhyme at the ends of lines.
   Re-read some of the earlier poems in this chapter, noting which ones
   contain internal rhyme° as well as external or end rhymes°. In some
   poems, the poet makes unusual combinations of words to achieve
   rhyme. What effects does the internal rhyme have? (Note especially
   *How the Helpmate of Blue-Beard Made Free with a Door*, p. 172.)

---

**Poems for Further Study**
These are some of the poems in Part One that contain good ex-
amples of rhyme used for various effects and purposes:
*The Unknown Citizen* (p. 15)
*If I Should Die To-Night* (p. 17)
*Acquainted With The Night* (p. 32)
*In Flanders Fields* (p. 48)
*I Have a Rendezvous With Death* (p. 49)
*There Will Come Soft Rains* (p. 51)
*Locksley Hall* (p. 55)
*Résumé* (p. 56)
*My Garden* (p. 77)
*O Earth, Turn!* (p. 98)

THE SOUNDS OF WORDS and even individual letters are important in poetry. Some sounds are associated with certain emotions. For example, surprise may be expressed by "Oooooooh" or "Aaaaah." Satisfaction or contentment may be expressed by "Mmmmmm," anger by "Sssss." Poets use sounds to contribute to the meanings of poems.

Some general uses of consonant sounds are the following:
- to suggest scorn or quickness of movement—b, p
- to suggest harshness, cruelty, noise or conflict—k, g, st, ts, ch
- to suggest humming, singing or music—m, m, ng
- to suggest peace, gentle motion, streams or rest—l

In general, long vowels are more peaceful and solemn, while short vowels suggest quick movement or agitation. By reading several poems, you will be able to classify other sounds yourself.

As you read these poems, note the sounds of the words, and see how the sounds relate to the meanings. But a word of warning about sounds: do not overstate their effects. Always consider sounds in relation to meaning. Some very pleasant sounds can have unpleasant meanings: moldy, cold oatmeal; diarrhea.

Note too that sound can be used with rhythm to speed up or slow down the reading of a line.

## DO NOT GO GENTLE
## INTO THAT GOOD NIGHT

Do not go gentle into that good night,
Old age should burn and rave at close of day;
Rage, rage against the dying of the light.

Though wise men at their end know dark is right,
Because their words had forked no lightning they          5
Do not go gentle into that good night.

Good men, the last wave by, crying how bright
Their frail deeds might have danced in a green bay,
Rage, rage against the dying of the light.

Wild men who caught and sang the sun in flight,          10
And learn, too late, they grieved it on its way,
Do not go gentle into that good night.

Grave men, near death, who see with blinding sight
Blind eyes could blaze like meteors and be gay,
Rage, rage against the dying of the light.          15

And you, my father, there on the sad height,

Curse, bless me now with your fierce tears, I pray.
Do not go gentle into that good night.
Rage, rage against the dying of the light.

DYLAN THOMAS (1914-1953)

## Questions

1. Notice the repetition of the first line of the poem and the line that ends the first stanza. How do the meanings, especially the connotations°, of these lines change and expand as the poem goes on?
2. What vowel and consonant sounds are used to create a feeling of struggle and anger?
3. Consider the imagery°, the metre and the sound of this poem; then decide if it is an effective statement. Give reasons for your opinion.

## STOPPING BY WOODS ON A SNOWY EVENING

Whose woods these are I think I know.
His house is in the village though;
He will not see me stopping here
To watch his woods fill up with snow.

My little horse must think it queer                               5
To stop without a farmhouse near
Between the woods and frozen lake
The darkest evening of the year.

He gives his harness bells a shake
To ask if there is some mistake.                                 10
The only other sound's the sweep
Of easy wind and downy flake.

The woods are lovely, dark and deep,
But I have promises to keep,
And miles to go before I sleep,
And miles to go before I sleep.

ROBERT FROST (1874-1963)

## Questions

This is one of the best loved and most often quoted modern poems.
1. How are rhythm and rhyme used? Do they seem natural or forced? Give reasons for your opinion.
2. What could account for the poem's popularity?

**Poems for Further Study**
Re-read these poems in Part One, noting the effects of the sounds of words:
*The Lonely Land* (p. 37)
*There Will Come Soft Rains* (p. 51)
*The Winter Lakes* (p. 77)
*To Autumn,* (p. 87)

# Poems for Interpretation

Only a few notes are given for the following poems. Read the poems carefully several times, especially noting the metre, the rhyme and other sound effects. Consider why they might be appropriate in each case. Then create your own questions for study and discussion.

### LOW TIDE ON GRANDE PRÉ

The sun goes down, and over all
These barren reaches by the tide
Such unelusive glories fall,
I almost dream they yet will bide
Until the coming of the tide.                    5

And yet I know that not for us,
By any ecstasy of dream,
He lingers to keep luminous
A little while the grievous stream,
Which frets, uncomforted of dream—              10

A grievous stream, that to and fro
Athrough the fields of Acadie
Goes wandering, as if to know
Why one beloved face should be
So long from home and Acadie.                    15

Was it a year or lives ago
We took the grasses in our hands,
And caught the summer flying low
Over the waving meadow lands,
And held it there between our hands?             20

The while the river at our feet—
A drowsy inland meadow stream—

At set of sun and after-heat
Made running gold, and in the gleam
We freed our birch upon the stream. 25

There down along the elms at dusk
We lifted dripping blade to drift,
Through twilight scented fine like musk,
Where night and gloom awhile uplift,
Nor sunder soul and soul adrift. 30

And that we took into our hands
Spirit of life or subtler thing—
Breathed on us here, and loosed the bands
Of death, and taught us, whispering,
The secrets of some wonder-thing. 35

Then all your face grew light, and seemed
To hold the shadow of the sun;
The evening faltered, and I deemed
That time was ripe, and years had done
Their wheeling underneath the sun. 40

So all desire and all regret,
And fear and memory, were naught;
One to remember or forget
The keen delight our hands had caught;
Morrow and yesterday were naught. 45

The night has fallen, and the tide ...
Now and again comes drifting home,
Across these aching barrens wide,
A sigh like driven wind or foam:
In grief the flood is bursting home. 50

BLISS CARMAN (1861-1929)

## Notes

*Grande Pré*: a village on the Minas Basin, Nova Scotia, settled by the Acadians in 1686.

*bide* (1.4): remain.

*luminous* (1.8): bright, full of light.

*athrough* (1.12): all through, throughout.

*Acadie* (1.12): French colony of Eastern Canada which extended over the territory of Nova Scotia, New Brunswick, Prince Edward Island and along the mainland coast from the Gulf of St. Lawrence to the northern reaches of Maine.

## THE SONG MY PADDLE SINGS

West wind, blow from your prairie nest,
Blow from the mountains, blow from the west.
The sail is idle, the sailor too;
O! wind of the west, we wait for you.
Blow, blow!                                                    5
I have wooed you so,
But never a favour you bestow.
You rock your cradle the hills between,
But scorn to notice my white lateen.

I stow the sail, unship the mast:                            10
I wooed you long but my wooing's past;
My paddle will lull you into rest.
O! drowsy wind of the drowsy west,
Sleep, sleep,
By your mountain steep,                                       15
Or down where the prairie grasses sweep!
Now fold in slumber your laggard wings,
For soft is the song my paddle sings.

August is laughing across the sky,
Laughing while paddle, canoe and I,                          20
Drift, drift,
Where the hills uplift
On either side of the current swift.

The river rolls in its rocky bed;
My paddle is plying its way ahead;                           25
Dip, dip,
While the waters flip
In foam as over their breast we slip.

And oh, the river runs swifter now;
The eddies circle about my bow,                              30
Swirl, swirl!
How the ripples curl
In many a dangerous pool awhirl!

And forward far the rapids roar,
Fretting their margin for evermore.                          35
Dash, dash,
With a mighty crash,
They seethe, and boil, and bound, and splash.

Be strong, O paddle! Be brave, canoe!
The reckless waves you must plunge into.                     40
Reel, reel.

On your trembling keel,
But never a fear my craft will feel.

We've raced the rapid, we're far ahead!
The river slips through its silent bed.                    45
Sway, sway,
As the bubbles spray
And fall in tinkling tunes away.

And up on the hills against the sky,
A fir tree rocking its lullaby,                            50
Swings, swings,
Its emerald wings,
Swelling the song that my paddle sings.

PAULINE JOHNSON (1862-1913)


**Notes**
*lateen* (l.9): triangular sail.
*laggard* (l.17): slow, with the connotation of laziness.

## "HOW THEY BROUGHT THE GOOD NEWS FROM GHENT TO AIX"

I sprang to the stirrup, and Joris, and he:
I galloped, Dirck galloped, we galloped all three;
"Good speed!" cried the watch, as the gatebolts undrew;
"Speed!" echoed the wall to us galloping through;
Behind shut the postern, the lights sank to rest,        5
And into the midnight we galloped abreast.

Not a word to each other; we kept the great pace
Neck by neck, stride by stride, never changing our place;
I turned in my saddle and made its girths tight,
Then shortened each stirrup, and set the pique right,     10
Rebuckled the cheek-strap, chained slacker the bit,
Nor galloped less steadily Roland a whit.

'Twas moonset at starting; but while we drew near
Lokeren, the cocks crew and twilight dawned clear;
At Boom, a great yellow star came out to see;            15
At Düffeld, 'twas morning as plain as could be;
And from Mecheln church-steeple we heard the half-chime,
So Joris broke silence with, "Yet there is time!"

At Aershot, up leaped of a sudden the sun,
And against him the cattle stood black every one,        20

To stare through the mist at us galloping past,
And I saw my stout galloper Roland at last,
With resolute shoulders, each butting away
The haze, as some bluff river headland its spray;

And his low head and crest, just one sharp ear bent back    25
For my voice, and the other pricked out on his track;
And one eye's black intelligence—ever that glance
O'er its white edge at me, his own master, askance!
And the thick heavy spume-flakes which aye and anon
His fierce lips shook upwards in galloping on.    30

By Hasselt, Dirck groaned; and cried Joris, "Stay spur!
Your Roos galloped bravely, the fault's not in her,
We'll remember at Aix"—for one heard the quick wheeze
Of her chest, saw the stretched neck and staggering knees,
And sunk tail, and horrible heave of the flank,    35
As down on her haunches she shuddered and sank.

So we were left galloping, Joris and I,
Past Looz and past Tongres, no cloud in the sky;
The broad sun above laughed a pitiless laugh,
'Neath our feet broke the brittle bright stubble like chaff;    40
Till over by Dalhem a dome-spire sprang white,
And "Gallop," gasped Joris, "for Aix is in sight!"

"How they'll greet us!"—and all in a moment his roan
Rolled neck and croup over, lay dead as a stone;
And there was my Roland to bear the whole weight    45
Of the news which alone could save Aix from her fate,
With his nostrils like pits full of blood to the brim,
And with circles of red for his eye-sockets' rim.

Then I cast loose my buffcoat, each holster let fall,
Shook off both my jack-boots, let go belt and all,    50
Stood up in the stirrup, leaned, patted his ear,
Called my Roland his pet-name, my horse without peer;
Clapped my hands, laughed and sang, any noise, bad or good,
Till at length into Aix Roland galloped and stood.

And all I remember is—friends flocking round    55
As I sat with his head 'twixt my knees on the ground;
And no voice but was praising this Roland of mine,
As I poured down his throat our last measure of wine,
Which (the burgesses voted by common consent)
Was no more than his due who brought good news from Ghent.

ROBERT BROWNING (1812-1889)

## Notes

*How They Brought the Good News ...*: The author stated that there was no historical basis for the poem. Ghent and Aix are cities in Belgium about 130 km (80 miles) apart.

*postern* (l.5): the rear gate.

*pique* (l.10): the pommel, the upward-pointing front part of the saddle.

*askance* (l.28): sideways.

*burgesses* (l.59): townspeople.

## THE KELLIGREWS' SOIREE

You may talk of Clara Nolan's Ball
    Or anything you choose,
But it couldn't hold a snuff-box
    To the spree of Kelligrews'.
If you want your eyeballs straightened,          5
    Just come out next week with me,
And you will have to wear your glasses
    At the Kelligrews' Soiree.

*Threre was birch rhine, tar twine,*
*Cherry wine and turpentine;*          10
    *Jowls and calavances, ginger beer and tea;*
*Pigs' feet, cats' meat, dumplin's boiled up in a sheet,*
*Dandelion and crackies teeth*
    *At the Kelligrews' Soiree.*

Oh, I borrowed Cluney's beaver          15
    As I squared my yards to sail,
And a swallow-tail from Hogan
    That was foxy on the tail;
Billy Cuddahie's old working pants,
    And Patsy Nowlan's shoes,          20
And an old white vest from Fogarty
    To sport in Kelligrews'.

*There was Dan Milley, Joe Lilly,*
*Tantan and Mrs. Tilley,*
*Dancing like a little filly,*          25
    *'Twould raise your heart to see,*
*Jim Brine, Din Ryan,*
    *Flipper Smith and Caroline;*
*I tell you, boys, we had a time*
    *At the Kelligrews' Soiree.*          30

Oh, when I arrived at Betsy Snooks'
    That night at half-past eight
The place was blocked with carriages
    Stood waiting at the gate;
With Cluney's funnel on my pate,                35
    The first word Betsy said,
"Here comes a local preacher
    With the pulpit on his head."

*There was Bill Mews, Dan Hughes,*
*Wilson, Taft, and Teddy Roose,*            40
*While Bryant he sat in the blues*
    *And looking hard at me;*
*Jim Fling, Tom King*
*And Johnson champion of the ring,*
*And all the boxers I could bring*        45
    *At the Kelligrews' Soiree.*

"The Saratoga Lancers first,"
    Miss Betsy kindly said;
Sure I danced with Nancy Cronan
    And her Grannie on the "Head";       50
And Hogan danced with Betsy;
    Oh, you should have seen his shoes
As he lashed old muskets from the rack
    That night in Kelligrews'.

*There was boiled guineas, cold guineas,*    55
*Bullocks' heads and piccaninnies*
*And everything to catch the pennies,*
    *You'd break your sides to see;*
*Boiled duff, cold duff,*
*Apple jam was in a cuff;*         60
*I tell you, boys, we had enough*
    *At the Kelligrews' Soiree.*

Cooked Flavin struck to the rim;
    And a hand I then took in.
You should see George Clooney's beaver    65
    And it flattened to the rim;
And Hogan's coat was like a vest—
    The tails were gone, you see;
"Oh," says I, "the devil haul ye
    And your Kelligrews' Soiree."       70

JOHN BURKE (1851-1933)

## Notes

*soiree*: evening party.

*calavances*: (l.11): vegetables such as peas and beans.

*swallow-tail* (l.17): type of coat with two-pointed skirt or tail.

*pate* (l.35): head, especially the crown.

*piccaninnies* (l.56): obsolete term for small children.

*duff* (l.59): a flour pudding.

# 3 THE FORMS POEMS TAKE

## Introduction

Poems can be classified in several ways, but no way is completely satisfactory. The way we classify poems depends on our point of view and on our purpose in classifying. We could look at a poem and say it is a love poem, or that it has five stanzas, or that it has a particular pattern of rhyme or metre, or that it was written by a certain poet, or that it is an example of the poetry of a certain time, etc.

In this chapter we will use a simple classification based on the poet's apparent purpose in writing the poem. Remember that these divisions or classifications are arbitrary and that many poems overlap the categories we use, while others may not even fit into them.

We may say that poems can be divided into three kinds: narrative°, lyric°, and didactic°.

- *Narrative poems* tell stories.
- *Lyric poems* express emotions and emotion-filled thoughts.
- *Didactic poems* usually explain ideas or state critical thoughts.

## Narrative Poems

Narrative poems tell of people involved in a sequence of important events. Like other narratives such as short stores and novels, narrative poems contain characters, a setting and a plot; they are based on conflict; and the events lead up to a climax. The structure of many narrative poems can be sketched as follows:

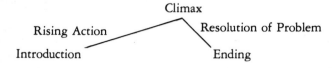

Climax

Rising Action          Resolution of Problem

Introduction          Ending

We will look at three forms of narrative poetry: the ballad°, the epic° and the dramatic monologue°.

THE BALLAD is perhaps the most popular type of narrative poem. It is usually a simple folk tale and is written in a verse form which you will pick up easily if you look at the following two examples.

## FRANKIE AND JOHNNY

Frankie and Johnny were lovers,
   Lordy, how they could love,
Swore to be true to each other,
    True as the stars up above,
      He was her man, but he done her wrong.      5

Frankie went down to the corner,
   To buy her a bucket of beer,
Frankie says "Mister Bartender,
    Has my lovin' Johnny been here?
      He is my man, but he's doing me wrong."    10

"I don't want to cause you no trouble
   Don't want to tell you no lie,
I saw your Johnny half-an-hour ago
    Making love to Nelly Bly.
      He is your man, but he's doing you wrong."   15

Frankie went down to the hotel
   Looked over the transom so high,
There she saw her lovin' Johnny
    Making love to Nelly Bly.
      He was her man; he was doing her wrong.   20

Frankie threw back her kimono,
   Pulled out her big forty-four;
Rooty-toot-toot: three times she shot
    Right through that hotel door,
      She shot her man, who was doing her wrong.   25

"Roll me over gently,
   Roll me over slow,
Roll me over on my right side,
    'Cause these bullets hurt me so,
      I was your man, but I done you wrong."   30

Bring all your rubber-tired hearses
   Bring all your rubber-tired hacks,

They're carrying poor Johnny to the burying ground
    And they ain't gonna bring him back,
        He was her man, but he done her wrong.      35

Frankie says to the sheriff,
    "What are they going to do?"
The sheriff he said to Frankie,
    "It's the 'lectric chair for you.
        He was your man, and he done you wrong."    40

"Put me in that dungeon,
    Put me in that cell,
Put me where the northeast wind
    Blows from the southeast corner of hell,
        I shot my man, 'cause he done me wrong."    45

AUTHOR UNKNOWN (19th century)

## Questions

1. Outline the plot of this poem according to the diagram on p. 177.
2. Where is repetition or near repetition used in the poem?
3. What is the dominant rhythm° of the poem? Why is that rhythm appropriate?

## LA BELLE DAME SANS MERCI

O what can ail thee, knight-at-arms!
    Alone and palely loitering!
The sedge has withered from the lake,
    And no birds sing.

O what can ail thee, knight-at-arms!      5
    So haggard and so woe-begone?
The squirrel's granary is full,
    And the harvest's done.

I see a lily on thy brow
    With anguish moist and fever dew,      10
And on thy cheeks a fading rose
    Fast withereth too.

"I met a lady in the meads,
    Full beautiful—a faery's child,
Her hair was long, her foot was light,      15
    And her eyes were wild.

"I made a garland for her head,
   And bracelets too, and fragrant zone;
She looked at me as she did love,
   And made sweet moan.                     20

"I set her on my pacing steed,
   And nothing else saw all day long.
For sidelong would she bend, and sing
   A faery's song.

"She found me roots of relish sweet,           25
   And honey wild and manna-dew;
And sure in language strange she said,
   'I love thee true.'

"She took me to her elfin grot,
   And there she wept and sighed full sore;     30
And there I shut her wild, wild eyes
   With kisses four.

"And there she lullèd me asleep,
   And there I dreamed—ah! woe betide!—
The latest dream I ever dreamed             35
   On the cold hillside.

"I saw pale kings, and princes too,
   Pale warriors, death-pale were they all:
They cried—'La Belle Dame sans Merci
   Hath thee in thrall!'                 40

"I saw their starved lips in the gloam
   With horrid warning gapèd wide,
And I woke, and found me here
   On the cold hillside.

"And this is why I sojourn here            45
   Alone and palely loitering,
Though the sedge is withered from the lake,
   And no birds sing."

JOHN KEATS (1795-1821)


## Notes

*La Belle Dame sans Merci*: The beautiful lady without pity.
*sedge* (l.3): coarse marsh grass.
*"I met a lady . . .* (l.13): The knight speaks from here to the end of the poem.

*zone* (l.18): waistband.

*manna-dew* (l.26): the food which nourished the Jews during their wanderings in the desert.

*grot* (l.29): grotto, a small cave (often used as a shrine).

*thrall* (l.40): under her spell.

*sojourn* (l.45): linger.

## Questions

1. Outline the plot of the poem.
2. How is this poem different from *Frankie and Johnny?*
3. Find some examples of repetition of words or phrases and of repetition of rhymes. What uses does the poet make of these repetitions?
4. What similarities in form are there in these two ballads?

---

**Ballads for Further Study**
*The Alberta Homesteader* (p. 7)
*The Banks of Newfoundland* (p. 9)
*Lost Jimmy Whelan* (p. 28)
*She's Like the Swallow* (p. 36)
*Annabel Lee* (p. 68)
*Canadian Railroad Trilogy* (p. 108)

---

THE EPIC is a narrative poem which tells of great heroes and events such as the building of the first transcontinental railway across Canada. An example of an epic poem is *The Titanic,* excerpts of which are the last poem in this chapter (p. 210).

THE DRAMATIC MONOLOGUE is a third type of narrative in which the story is revealed by the words of a single character in the poem. There is often another character present who does not speak. Two examples of dramatic monologue in Part One are *What Do I Remember of the Evacuation* (p. 48) and *Dover Beach* (p. 79).

# Lyric Poems

Lyric poems° are usually short and express a single feeling, mood or emotion. One of the most popular emotions expressed in the lyric is love: But sadness is expressed in some types of lyric poetry, and other emotions may also be present. Lyric poems are often stated in the first person (e.g. *How do I love thee?*, p. 24) and are usually thoughtful, expressing little physical action.

THE SONNET° is among the most popular of lyric forms. The sonnet has fourteen lines and usually expresses one main idea. You can discover more about the sonnet by reading a few in the following group of poems.

THE ODE° is usually longer than other lyrics. It often expresses serious thoughts or reflections on a topic, and it is usually stated in elevated language.

THE ELEGY° usually expresses sad thoughts, often on the subject of death.

There are several other types of lyric poems, but these three are the most common and will serve as an introduction to other kinds.

Lyric poems have a variety of structures. As you read lyric poems, look for the development of the poet's thought. Often you can identify the main idea in each stanza or in each section of the poem. These main ideas will give you an outline of the thought. The parts of the poem are often identified by the rhyme scheme° or by patterns of images.

### YOUNG GIRLS

With the night full of spring and stars we stand
here in this dark doorway and watch the young
girls pass, two, three together, hand in hand.
Like flowers they are whose fragrance has not sprung
or awakened, whose bodies dimly feel                                5
the flooding upward welling of the trees;
whose senses, caressed by the wind's soft fingers, reel
with a delirium that makes them ill at ease.
They lie awake at night unable to sleep
and walk the streets kindled by strange desires;           10
they steal glances at us, unable to keep
control upon those subterranean fires.
We whistle after them, then laugh, for they
stiffen, not knowing what to do or say.

RAYMOND SOUSTER (b. 1921)

Questions
1. Who might be the speaker° of these words?
2. In what way is this a love poem?
3. Note the rhyme scheme of the poem. What connections are there between the rhyme and the development of the thought?


## WHAT LIPS MY LIPS HAVE KISSED

What lips my lips have kissed, and where, and why,
I have forgotten, and what arms have lain
Under my head till morning; but the rain
Is full of ghosts tonight, that tap and sigh
Upon the glass and listen for reply;                          5
And in my heart there stirs a quiet pain
For unremembered lads that not again
Will turn to me at midnight with a cry.

Thus in the winter stands the lonely tree,
Nor knows what birds have vanished one by one,          10
Yet knows its boughs more silent than before:
I cannot say what loves have come and gone;
I only know that summer sang in me
A little while, that in me sings no more.

EDNA ST. VINCENT MILLAY (1892-1950)


Questions
1. What characteristics of lyric poetry are contained in this poem?
2. What are some effective uses of figurative language° in the poem?
3. Describe the rhythm and rhyme of the poem. What do these devices contribute to the poem?


## ODE TO A NIGHTINGALE

My heart aches, and a drowsy numbness pains
    My sense, as though of hemlock I had drunk,
Or emptied some dull opiate to the drains
    One minute past, and Lethe-wards had sunk:
'Tis not through envy of thy happy lot,                       5
    But being too happy in thine happiness,—
        That thou, light-wingèd Dryad of the trees,
            In some melodious plot

Of beechen green, and shadows numberless,
   Singest of summer in full-throated ease.        10

O for a draught of vintage, that hath been
   Cool'd a long age in the deep-delvèd earth,
Tasting of Flora and the country green,
   Dance, and Provençal song, and sun-burnt mirth!
O for a beaker full of the warm South,        15
   Full of the true, the blushful Hippocrene,
      With beaded bubbles winking at the brim,
         And purple-stainèd mouth;
   That I might drink and leave the world unseen,
      And with thee fade away into the forest dim:      20

Fade far away, dissolve, and quite forget
   What thou among the leaves hast never known,
The weariness, the fever, and the fret
   Here, where men sit and hear each other groan;
Where palsy shakes a few, sad, last grey hairs,     25
   Where youth grows pale, and spectre-thin, and dies;
      Where but to think is to be full of sorrow
         And leaden-eyed despairs;
   Where Beauty cannot keep her lustrous eyes,
      Or new Love pine at them beyond to-morrow.     30

Away! away! for I will fly to thee,
   Not charioted by Bacchus and his pards,
But on the viewless wings of Poesy,
   Though the dull brain perplexes and retards:
Already with thee! tender is the night,       35
   And haply the Queen-Moon is on her throne,
      Cluster'd around by all her starry Fays;
        But here there is no light,
   Save what from heaven is with the breezes blown
      Through verdurous glooms and winding mossy ways. 40

I cannot see what flowers are at my feet,
   Nor what soft incense hangs upon the boughs,
But, in embalmèd darkness, guess each sweet
   Wherewith the seasonable month endows
The grass, the thicket, and the fruit-tree wild;     45
   White hawthorn, and the pastoral eglantine;
      Fast-fading violets cover'd up in leaves;
         And mid-May's eldest child,
   The coming musk-rose, full of dewy wine,
      The murmurous haunt of flies on summer eves.    50

Darkling I listen; and for many a time
I have been half in love with easeful Death,
Call'd him soft names in many a musèd rhyme,
To take into the air my quiet breath;
Now more than ever seems it rich to die,          55
To cease upon the midnight with no pain,
While thou art pouring forth thy soul abroad
In such an ecstasy!
Still wouldst thou sing, and I have ears in vain—
To thy high requiem become a sod.          60

Thou wast not born for death, immortal Bird!
No hungry generations tread thee down;
The voice I hear this passing night was heard
In ancient days by emperor and clown:
Perhaps the self-same song that found a path          65
Through the sad heart of Ruth, when sick for home,
She stood in tears amid the alien corn;
The same that oft-times hath
Charm'd magic casements, opening on the foam
Of perilous seas, in faery lands forlorn.          70

Forlorn! the very word is like a bell
To toll me back from thee to my sole self!
Adieu! the fancy cannot cheat so well
As she is fam'd to do, deceiving elf,
Adieu! adieu! thy plaintive anthem fades          75
Past the near meadows, over the still stream,
Up the hill-side; and now 'tis buried deep
In the next valley-glades:
Was it a vision, or a waking dream?
Fled is that music:—Do I wake or sleep?          80

JOHN KEATS (1795-1821)


## Notes

*hemlock* (1.2): a drug made from the poisonous hemlock plant.
*Lethe-wards* (1.4): towards Lethe, the river of forgetfulness in Hades.
*Dryad* (1.7): a tree nymph.
*Flora* (1.13): The goddess of flowers and the spring.
*Provençal song* (1.14): Provence: a district in France said to be the home of wandering singers.
*Hippocrene* (1.16): a fountain on Mount Helicon sacred to the Muses.

*Bacchus* (l.32): the god of wine, often shown riding in a carriage drawn by leopards (pards) or tigers.
*viewless* (l.33): invisible.
*Fays* (l.37): fairies.
*verdurous* (l.40): green and fresh.
*embalmèd* (l.43): balmy, fragrant.

### Questions

1. Re-read the poem and state the main point of each stanza, using one sentence for each.
2. How is the language of this ode different from that of the lyric poems? How is the theme° different?
3. What is the dominant tone° of the poem? How is that tone created?

Another ode by Keats appears in Part One: *To Autumn* (p. 87).

## ELEGY WRITTEN IN A COUNTRY CHURCHYARD
*—an excerpt*

The curfew tolls the knell of parting day,
   The lowing herd winds slowly o'er the lea,
The plowman homeward plods his weary way,
   And leaves the world to darkness and to me.

Now fades the glimm'ring landscape on the sight,     5
   And all the air a solemn stillness holds,
Save where the beetle wheels his droning flight,
   And drowsy tinklings lull the distant folds;

Save that from yonder ivy-mantled tow'r
   The moping owl does to the moon complain     10
Of such, as wand'ring near her secret bow'r,
   Molest her ancient solitary reign.

Beneath those rugged elms, that yew-tree's shade,
   Where heaves the turf in many a mould'ring heap,
Each in his narrow cell for ever laid,     15
   The rude forefathers of the hamlet sleep

THOMAS GRAY (1716-1771)

### Notes

*curfew* (l.1): a bell rung as a signal to extinguish fires in the evening; a signal that the day is ending.
*moping* (l.10): gloomy, sulking.

**Questions**
1. These stanzas are the first four of a longer poem which is a detailed meditation on death. Describe the general movement of these lines. How are rhythm and sound used to create this movement? Why is this movement appropriate?
2. What images relate especially well to the feeling and tone created by the metre° and sound?
3. What theme about death does the poem state?

---

**Lyric Poems for Further Study**
*Our Daily Death* (p. 11)
*First Person Demonstrative* (p. 24)
*Memory* (p. 26)

---

# Didactic Poems

Didactic poetry° is usually written to teach or to state an informative message. The theme in a didactic poem is usually much easier to find than it is in a narrative or lyric poem. Didactic poems may make a comment on society, explain an event or topic, or make other critical comments. When a poem makes critical comments in a humorous way, it is called a satiric poem°.

It is often hard to tell if a poem is didactic or lyric. Sometimes a poem can teach a lesson by expressing an emotion and by creating the same emotion in the reader; sometimes a lesson can be taught by telling a story. The reader must decide if the poem is didactic, lyric or narrative. Generally, if the main purpose seems to be to explain, the poem is didactic; if the main purpose is to express an emotion, it is lyric; if it seems to tell a story, it is narrative.

To find the structure of a didactic poem look for the main thought in each stanza or major part of the poem. Listing the main thoughts will give an outline of the poet's argument or explanation. As with lyric poems, these divisions are often marked by the rhyme scheme or by patterns of images.

## A POISON TREE

I was angry with my friend:
I told my wrath, my wrath did end.
I was angry with my foe:
I told it not, my wrath did grow.

And I watered it in fears                                    5
Night and morning with my tears,
And I sunnèd it with smiles
And with soft deceitful wiles.

And it grew both day and night,
Till it bore an apple bright,                                10
And my foe beheld it shine,
And he knew that it was mine—

And into my garden stole
When the night had veiled the pole;
In the morning, glad, I see                                  15
My foe outstretched beneath the tree.

WILLIAM BLAKE (1757-1827)


## Questions

1. What moral or lesson is contained in this poem?
2. What are the connotations° of the words "apple" and "garden"?
3. What metaphor° gives the poem unity°? How is the metaphor extended?
4. State in everyday language the meaning of the images in stanza two.


---

**Didactic Poems for Further Study**
*South Viewed by North American Eskimo* (p. 96)
*The Blind Men and the Elephant* (p. 112)

# Closed and Open Forms

In the poems that you have read so far, you have noticed that some follow regular patterns of rhyme and rhythm while others do not. Poems which have a regular metre, rhyme scheme or structure are said to be in closed form°. That type of poem must be written in that particular way. Poems which follow no regular patterns are in open form°. Poets choose the form which seems most appropriate for each poem they write. Think of *form* as the design or pattern of the poem as a whole. Every poem has some form.

CLOSED FORM poetry is traditional, and you will find examples of its many variations in the work of less recent poets. A good example of the closed form is the *sonnet*. Examine the sonnets below and find their forms by answering these questions:
- How many lines are there in the poem?
- In what metre are the lines written?
- What is the rhyme pattern of the poem?
- Into how many parts does the rhyme divide the poem?

By putting together your answers to these questions and adding insights of your own, you will have a good description of two sonnet forms.

### LET ME NOT TO THE MARRIAGE OF TRUE MINDS
*from Sonnets, CXVI*

Let me not to the marriage of true minds
Admit impediments. Love is not love
Which alters when it alteration finds,
Or bends with the remover to remove:
O, no! it is an ever-fixèd mark,                                    5
That looks on tempests and is never shaken;
It is the star to every wand'ring bark,
Whose worth's unknown, although his height be taken.
Love's not Time's fool, though rosy lips and cheeks
Within his bending sickle's compass come;                          10
Love alters not with his brief hours and weeks,
But bears it out even to the edge of doom:—
    If this be error and upon me proved,
    I never writ, nor no man ever loved.

WILLIAM SHAKESPEARE (1564-1616)

**Notes**
*mark* (l.5): a landmark used by sailors for guidance.

*bark* (l.7): a small boat.
*his bending sickle's compass* (l.10): Time's curved sickle's range; a traditional symbol of time is an old man with a sickle.
*bears it out* (l.12): endures.

## LOVE'S INCONSISTENCY

I find no peace, and all my war is done;
  I fear and hope, I burn and freeze likewise;
  I fly above the wind, yet cannot rise;
  And nought I have, yet all the world I seize on;
That looseth, nor locketh, holdeth me in prison,        5
  And holds me not, yet can I 'scape no wise;
  Nor lets me live, nor die, at my devise,
  And yet of death it giveth none occasion.
Without eyes I see, and without tongue I plain;
  I wish to perish, yet I ask for health;        10
  I love another, and yet I hate myself;
I feed in sorrow, and laugh in all my pain;
  Lo, thus displeaseth me both death and life,
  And my delight is causer of my grief.

FRANCESCO PETRARCA (1304-1324)
*Translated by*
SIR THOMAS WYATT (1503-1542)

## Notes
*nought* (l.4): nothing.
*that* (l.5): that which.
*plain* (l.9): explain, speak.

## Questions
1. How are the two sonnet forms alike?
2. How are they different?

## • Being Aware of the Sonnet Form
Now re-read the sonnets, *Young Girls* (p. 183) and *What My Lips Have
Kissed* (p. 184).
1. Compare the forms of the poems. What similarities and differences are there in
   a) rhyme and rhythm
   b) the divisions of thought?
2. What connections do you find between rhythm, rhyme and
   thought?

**Sonnets for Further Study**
There are several sonnets on various themes in Part One. Some of them are:
*On His Blindness* (p. 6)
*Death, Be Not Proud* (p. 13)
*Ozymandias* (p. 14)
*How Do I Love Thee?* (p. 24)
*Dreamers* (p. 46)
*Anthem For Doomed Youth* (p. 47)
*When In Disgrace With Fortune and Men's Eyes* (p. 53)
*High Flight* (p. 97)

Another closed form, perhaps second in popularity only to the sonnet, is the *limerick°*. Read the selections that follow, and answer the questions about the limerick that you have answered about the sonnet (p. 192).

What generalizations can you make about the sense, feeling, tone and intention of the limerick form? What does the form itself contribute to these meanings?

## LIMERICKS

I sat next to the Duchess at tea.
It was just as I thought it would be:
 Her rumblings abdominal
 Were simply phenomenal
And everyone thought it was me.

   \* \* \*

There once was a pious young priest
Who lived almost wholly on yeast.
 He said, "It's so plain
 We must all rise again
That I'd like to get started at least."

   \* \* \*

There was a young lady of Niger,
Who smiled as she rode on a tiger.
 They returned from the ride
 With the lady inside,
And the smile on the face of the tiger.

Both the sonnet and the limerick are one stanza poems. Poems of more than one stanza may also follow certain patterns. The *ballad*, for example, traditionally is made up of several four-line stanzas with an *abcb* rhyme pattern. The first and third lines of each stanza usually have four stressed syllables, while the second and fourth lines have three. Some other closed forms are the *ode*° and the *epigram*°, which are defined in the glossary.

---

**Epigrams for Further Study**
*Preparedness* (p. 6)
*Outwitted* (p. 55)
*Résumé* (p. 56)

---

OPEN FORM poetry has become very popular in the twentieth century. While poets have always experimented with different forms, it is only recently that many have felt that variations on the old forms have been exhausted and that new forms must be found. Some feel that the rapid social and cultural changes that are occurring in the modern world cannot be expressed in the old forms. A new world demands new forms of expression. Others believe that poems should have a feeling of spontaneity, that the words and ideas must find their own form as the poem is created.

Closed forms use rhythm and rhyme for emphasis. In open forms, the the poet makes greater use of white space and of line length to achieve emphasis. White space on a page causes us to pause, however briefly. In open forms, the poet groups words for their visual effects, often setting single words off where they will stand out.

Line length is important in both closed and open forms, but in open forms line divisions are often divisions of thoughts. We tend to pause at the end of each line, thereby pausing to consider the thought.

Because open forms have no metre or rhyme, some people think they are easier to write. But they may actually be harder to write because poets must use fewer devices to achieve desired effects. In the last chapter, we saw some of the uses of rhyme and metre. Writers in open form do not have these devices to work with so must find other methods to achieve those effects. Also, by working in a closed form poets often discover language, expressions, ideas and relationships that they would not have thought of otherwise because of the constraints imposed by the poem's rhythm and rhyme. When working in open form, poets must simply find the right words and may actually be more limited in the flow of ideas. W. H. Auden has compared the poet working in open form to Robinson Crusoe, who had to find out and do everything for himself.

As you read the following poem, try to answer these questions:

- How does the poet achieve emphasis on important ideas and words?
- How is the overall form or structure of the poem made clear to the reader?

Add some other insights of your own about open forms of poetry.

### th tomato conspiracy aint worth a whol pome

```
              very few peopul
       realize ths but altho yu have 5 or 6
    billyun peopul walking around beleeving

    that tomatoez ar red    they ar
         actually blu    nd ar sprayd              5
    red to make ther apperance
         consistent with peopuls beleef

         i was whuns inside th
      largest tomato spraying plant
    in th world with binoculars nd               10
      camoflage material all ovr me

         nd ive got th pictures to proov it
      oranges uv corz ar not orange nor ar lemons
         lemon color    its all a marage    it

    was decreed what color things                15
       wud b at th beginning nd then
          theyve bin colord that
             way evr since

                it adds to th
       chemicals nd artifishulness uv everything   20
    we eet tho did yu know that oranges
       ar actually a discouraging off
             color

         i was luky really to get
    out uv th tomato factoree alive              25
       th tomatoez wer really
             upset to b xposed
```

BILL BISSETT (b. 1939)

## Questions

1. In spite of the unusual form, you probably had little trouble understanding the poem. How did the poet cause us to pause at the right places and to understand the words although they were misspelled? That is, what did the poet substitute for traditional spelling and punctuation?
2. Why do you think the poet chose this form? Consider speaker, situation and audience.
3. What do you think are the theme and intent of the poem? Did the poet achieve his purpose? Give reasons for your opinion.

---

**Open Form Poems for Further Study**
There are many examples of poems in open forms in Part One. Some of them are:

*Chronology* (p. 4)

*Greetings From the Incredible Shrinking Woman* (p. 5)

*Our Daily Death* (p. 11)

*The Chance-Taking Dead* (p. 17)

*First Person Demonstrative* (p. 24)

*Memory* (p. 26)

*Someone Who Used to Have Someone* (p. 31)

*Agatha Christie* (p. 45)

*I Have a Rendezvous With Death* (p. 49)

---

# Poems For Interpretation

As you read through the poems below, identify them by form, and see if you can discover any similarities in the content or imagery within forms. For example: are there certain images that frequently occur in sonnets? Do narratives have any recurring patterns?

## THE RAVEN

Once upon a midnight dreary, while I pondered, weak and weary,
Over many a quaint and curious volume of forgotten lore—
While I nodded, nearly napping, suddenly there came a tapping,
As of some one gently rapping, rapping at my chamber door.

"'Tis some visitor," I muttered, "tapping at my chamber door—    5
   Only this and nothing more."

Ah, distinctly I remember it was in the Bleak December;
And each separate dying ember wrought its ghost upon the floor.
Eagerly I wished the morrow;—vainly I had sought to borrow
From my books surcease of sorrow—sorrow for the lost Lenore—    10
For the rare and radiant maiden whom the angels name Lenore—
   Nameless *here* for evermore.

And the silken, sad, uncertain rustling of each purple curtain
Thrilled me—filled me with fantastic terrors never felt before;
So that now, to still the beating of my heart, I stood repeating    15
"'Tis some visitor entreating entrance at my chamber door—
Some late visitor entreating entrance at my chamber door;—
   This it is and nothing more."

Presently my soul grew stronger; hesitating then no longer,
"Sir," said I, "or Madam, truly your forgiveness I implore;    20
But the fact is I was napping, and so gently you came rapping,
And so faintly you came tapping, tapping at my chamber door,
That I scarce was sure I heard you"—here I opened wide the door;
   Darkness there and nothing more.

Deep into that darkness peering, long I stood there wondering,
   fearing,    25
Doubting, dreaming dreams no mortal ever dared to dream before;
But the slience was unbroken, and the stillness gave no token,
And the only word there spoken was the whispered word, "Lenore!"
This I whispered, and an echo murmured back the word "Lenore!"
   Merely this and nothing more.    30

Back into the chamber turning, all my soul within me burning,
Soon again I heard a tapping somewhat louder than before.
"Surely," said I, "surely that is something at my window lattice;
Let me see, then, what thereat is, and this mystery explore—
Let my heart be still a moment and this mystery explore;—    35
   'Tis the wind and nothing more!"

Open here I flung the shutter, when, with many a flirt and flutter
In there stepped a stately Raven of the saintly days of yore.
Not the least obeisance made he; not a minute stopped or stayed he;
But, with mien of lord or lady, perched above my chamber door—    40
Perched upon a bust of Pallas just above my chamber door—
   Perched, and sat, and nothing more.

Then this ebony bird beguiling my sad fancy into smiling,
By the grave and stern decorum of the countenance it wore,

"Though thy crest be shorn and shaven, thou," I said, "art sure no
    craven,                                                45
Ghastly grim and ancient Raven wandering from the Nightly shore—
Tell me what thy lordly name is on the Night's Plutonian shore!"
    Quoth the Raven, "Nevermore."

Much I marvelled this ungainly fowl to hear discourse so plainly,
Though its answer little meaning—little relevancy bore;         50
For we cannot help agreeing that no living human being
Ever yet was blessed with seeing bird above his chamber door—
Bird or beast upon the sculptured bust above his chamber door,
    With such name as "Nevermore."

But the Raven, sitting lonely on the placid bust, spoke only     55
That one word, as if his soul in that one word he did outpour.
Nothing farther then he uttered—not a feather then he fluttered—
Till I scarcely more than muttered "Other friends have flown before—
On the morrow *he* will leave me, as my hopes have flown before."
    Then the bird said "Nevermore."                      60

Startled at the stillness broken by reply so aptly spoken,
"Doubtless," said I, "what it utters is its only stock and store
Caught from some unhappy master whom unmerciful Disaster
Followed fast and followed faster till his songs one burden bore—
Till the dirges of his Hope that melancholy burden bore
    Of 'Never—nevermore.' "                         65

But the Raven still beguiling all my fancy into smiling,
Straight I wheeled a cushioned seat in front of bird, and bust and door;
Then, upon the velvet sinking, I betook myself to linking
Fancy unto fancy, thinking what this ominous bird of yore—
What this grim, ungainly, ghastly, gaunt, and ominous bird of yore   70
    Meant in croaking "Nevermore."

This I sat engaged in guessing, but no syllable expressing
To the fowl whose fiery eyes now burned into my bosom's core;
This and more I sat divining, with my head at ease reclining
On the cushion's velvet lining that the lamp-light gloated o'er,     75
But whose velvet violet lining with the lamp-light gloating o'er,
    *She* shall press, ah, nevermore!

Then, methought, the air grew denser, perfumed from an unseen censer
Swung by Seraphim whose foot-falls tinkled on the tufted floor.
"Wretch," I cried, "thy God hath lent thee—by these angels he hath sent
    thee                                              80
Respite—respite and nepenthe from thy memories of Lenore;
Quaff, oh quaff this kind nepenthe and forget this lost Lenore!"
    Quoth the Raven "Nevermore."

"Prophet!" said I, "thing of evil! prophet still, if bird or devil!—
Whether Tempter sent, or whether tempest tossed thee here
    ashore,                                                   85
Desolate yet all undaunted, on this desert land enchanted—
On this home by Horror haunted—tell me truly, I implore—
Is there—*is* there balm in Gilead?—tell me—tell me, I implore!"
    Quoth the Raven "Nevermore."

"Prophet!" said I, "thing of evil!—prophet still, if bird or devil!   90
By that Heaven that bends above us—by that God we both adore—
Tell this soul with sorrow laden if, within the distant Aidenn,
It shall clasp a sainted maiden whom the angels name Lenore—
Clasp a rare and radiant maiden whom the angels name Lenore."
    Quoth the Raven "Nevermore."                                   95

"Be that word our sign of parting, bird or fiend!" I shrieked, up-starting—
"Get thee back into the tempest and the Night's Plutonian shore!
Leave no black plume as a token of that lie thy soul hath spoken!
Leave my loneliness unbroken!—quit the bust above my door!
Take thy beak from out my heart, and take thy form from off my
    door!"                                              100
    Quoth the Raven "Nevermore."

And the Raven, never flitting, Still is sitting, *still* is sitting
On the pallid bust of Pallas just above my chamber door;
And his eyes have all the seeming of a demon's that is dreaming,
And the lamp-light o'er him streaming throws his shadow on the
    floor;                                              105
And my soul from out that shadow that lies floating on the floor
    Shall be lifted—nevermore!

EDGAR ALLAN POE (1809-1849)

## Notes

*obeisance* (l.39): gesture of respect, e.g. a bow or salute.

*mien* (l.40): manner of movement.

*Pallas* (l.41): Greek goddess of wisdom, Pallas Athena.

*Plutonian* (l.47): 'Pluto' is both the name of a planet and the Latin name
    for the lord of Hades (Hell).

*Seraphim* (l.79): a heavenly choir of angels.

*Nepenthe* (l.81): an ancient drug that caused forgetfulness.

*balm in Gilead* (l.88): an herbal medicine used since Biblical times; the
    words used here are similar to a cry of sorrow of the prophet Jeremiah;
    he is asking if there will be relief from his suffering.

*Aidenn* (l.92): the Babylonian name for paradise, the Garden of Eden.

## WHAT TROUBLED POE'S RAVEN

Could Poe walk again to-morrow, heavy with dyspeptic sorrow,
While the darkness seemed to borrow darkness from the night
before,
From the hollow gloom abysmal, floating downward, grimly
dismal,
Like a pagan curse baptismal from the bust above the door,
He would hear the Raven croaking from the dusk above the
door,                                                              5
  "Never, never, nevermore!"

And, too angry to be civil, "Raven," Poe would cry "or
devil,
Tell me why you will persist in haunting Death's Plutonian
shore?"
Then would croak the Raven gladly, "I will tell you why so
sadly,
I so mournfully and madly, haunt you, taunt you, o'er and
o'er—                                                             10
Why eternally I haunt you, daunt you, taunt you, o'er
and o'er,
  Only this, and nothing more.

"Forty-eight long years I've pondered, forty-eight long years
I've wondered,
How a poet ever blundered into a mistake so sore.
How could lamp-light from your table ever in the world be
able,                                                             15
From *below*, to throw my sable shadow 'streaming on the
floor,'
When I perched up here on Pallas, high above your chamber-
door?
  Tell me that—if nothing more!"

Then, like some wan, weeping willow, Poe would bend above
his pillow,
Seeking surcease in the billow where mad recollections
drown,                                                            20
And in tearful tones replying, he would groan "There's no
denying
Either I was blindly lying, or the world was upside down—
Say, by Joe!—it was just midnight—so the world *was* upside
down—
  Aye, the world was upside down!"

JOHN BENNETT

## Notes

*What Troubled Poe's Raven*: Note the elements of form, rhyme, rhythm
and feeling that this poem retains from Poe's original.

*dyspeptic* (l.1): gloomy, pessimistic (also meaning poor digestion).

*surcease* (l.20): relief, an end to trouble.

## THE ICE FLOES

Dawn from the Fore-top! Dawn from the Barrel!
A scurry of feet with a roar overhead;
A master-watch wildly pointing to Northward,
Where the herd in front of the Eagle was spread!
Steel-planked and sheathed like a battleship's nose,     5
She battered her path through the drifting floes;
Past slob and growler we drove, and rammed her.
Into the heart of the patch and jammed her.
There were hundreds of thousands of seals, I'd swear,
In the stretch of that field—"white harps" to spare     10
For a dozen such fleets as had left that spring
To share in the general harvesting.
The first of the line, we had struck the main herd;
The day was ours, and our pulses stirred
In that brisk, live hour before the sun,     15
At the thought of the load and the sweepstake won.

We stood on the deck as the morning outrolled
On the fields its tissue of orange and gold,
And lit up the ice to the north in the sharp,
Clear air; each mother-seal and its "harp"     20
Lay side by side; and as far as the range
Of the patch ran out we saw that strange,
And unimaginable thing
That sealers talk of every spring—
The "bobbing-holes" within the floes     25
That neither wind nor frost could close;
Through every hole a seal could dive,
And search, to keep her brood alive,
A hundred miles it well might be,
For food beneath that frozen sea.     30
Round sunken reef and cape she would rove,
And though the ice and current drove
The ice-fields many leagues that day,
We knew she would turn and find her way
Back to the hole, without the help     35

Of compass or log, to suckle her whelp—
Back to that hole in the distant floes,
And smash her way up with teeth and nose.
But we flung those thoughts aside when the shout
Of command from the master-watch rang out.          40
Assigned to our places in watches of four—
Over the rails in a wild carouse,
Two from the port and the starboard bows,
Two from the broadside—off we tore,
In the breathless rush for the day's attack,          45
With the speed of hounds on a caribou's track.

With the rise of the sun we started to kill,
A seal for each blow from the iron bill
Of our gaffs. From the nose to the tail we ripped them,
And laid their quivering carcasses flat          50
On the ice; then with our knives we stripped them
For the sake of the pelt and its lining of fat.
With three fathoms of rope we laced them fast,
With their skins to the ice to be easy to drag,
With our shoulders galled we drew them, and cast          55
Them in thousands around the watch's flag.
Then, with our bodies begrimed with the reek
Of grease and sweat from the toil of the day,
We made for the Eagle, two miles away,
At the signal that flew from her mizzen-peak.          60
And through the night, as inch by inch
She reached the pans with the harps piled high,
We hoisted them up as the hours filed by
To the sleepy growl of the donkey-winch.

Over the bulwarks again we were gone,          65
With the first faint streaks of a misty dawn;
Fast as our arms could swing we slew them,
Ripped them, "sculped" them, roped, and drew them
To the pans where the seals in pyramids rose
Around the flags on the central floes,          70
Till we reckoned we had nine thousand dead
By the time the afternoon had fled;
And that an added thousand or more
Would beat the count of the day before.
So back again to the patch we went          75
To haul, before the day was spent,
Another load of four "harps" a man,
To make the last the record pan.
And not one of us saw, as we gaffed and skinned

And took them in tow, that the north-east wind        80
Had veered off-shore; that the air was colder;
That the signs of recall were there to the south,
The flag of the Eagle, and the long, thin smoulder
That drifted away from her funnel's mouth.
Not one of us thought of the speed of the storm        85
That hounded our tracks in the day's last chase
(For the slaughter was swift, and the blood was warm),
Till we felt the first sting of the snow in our face.

We looked south-east, where, an hour ago,
Like a smudge on the sky-line, someone had seen        90
The Eagle, and thought he had heard her blow
A note like a warning from her sirene.
We gathered in knots, each man within call
Of his mate, and slipping our ropes, we sped,
Plunging our way through a thickening wall        95
Of snow that the gale was driving ahead.
We ran with the wind on our shoulder; we knew
That the night had left us this only clue
Of the track before us, though with each wail
That grew to the pang of a shriek from the gale,        100
Some of us swore that the Eagle screamed
Right off to the east; to others it seemed
On the southern quarter and near, while the rest
Cried out with every report that rose
From the strain and the rend of the wind on the floes        105
That the Eagle was firing her guns to the west.
And some of them turned to the west, though to go
Was madness—we knew it and roared; but the notes
Of our warning were lost as a fierce gust of snow
Eddied, and strangled the words in our throats.        110
Then we felt in our hearts that the night had swallowed
All signals, the whistle, the flare, and the smoke
To the south; and like sheep in a storm we followed
Each other; like sheep we huddled and broke.

Here one would fall as hunger took hold        115
Of his step; here one would sleep as the cold
Crept into his blood, another would kneel
Athwart the body of some dead seal,
And with knife and nails would tear it apart,
To flesh his teeth in its frozen heart.        120
And another dreamed that the storm was past,
And raved of his bunk and brandy and food,
And the Eagle near, though in that blast

The mother was fully as blind as her brood.
Then we saw what we feared from the first—dark places 125
Here and there to the left of us, wide, yawning spaces
Of water; the fissures and cracks had increased
Till the outer pans were afloat, and we knew,
As they drifted along in the night to the east,
By the cries we heard, that some of our crew 130
Were borne to the sea on those pans and were lost.
And we turned with the wind in our faces again,
And took the snow with its lancing pain,
Till our eyebrows cracked with the salt and the frost;
Till only iron and fire that night 135
Survived on the ice as we stumbled on;
As we fell and rose and plunged—till the light
In the south and east disclosed the dawn,
And the sea heaving with floes—and then,
The Eagle in wild pursuit of her men. 140
And the rest is as a story told,
Of a dream that belonged to a dim, mad past,
Of a March night and a north wind's cold,
Of a voyage home with a flag half-mast;
Of twenty thousand seals that were killed 145
To help to lower the price of bread;
Of the muffled beats . . . of a drum . . . that filled
A nave . . . at our count of sixty dead.

E.J. PRATT (1882-1964)


**Notes**
*carouse* (l.42): a wild, noisy party.
*gaffs* (l.49): hooks, barbed spears.
*galled* (l.55): made sore by rubbing.


## THE SONNET

A sonnet is a moment's monument—
Memorial from the Soul's eternity
To one dead deathless hour. Look that it be,
Whether for lustral rite or dire portent,
Of its own arduous fullness reverent. 5
Carve it in ivory or in ebony,
As Day or Night may rule; and let Time see
Its flowering crest impearled and orient.

A sonnet is a coin; its face reveals
The Soul—its converse, to what Power 'tis due:—          10
Whether for tribute to the august appeals
Of Life, or dower in Love's high retinue,
It serve; or 'mid the dark wharf's cavernous breath,
In Charon's palm it pay the toll to Death.

DANTE GABRIEL ROSSETTI (1828-1882)

**Notes**

*lustral rite* (l.4): ceremony of purification.

*Charon* (l.14): in mythology, the boatman who ferries the souls of the dead
across the river Styx to Hades (the Underworld). His pay (toll) was a
coin in the mouth of the passenger.

## AN ELEGY ON THE DEATH OF A MAD DOG

Good people all, of every sort,
    Give ear unto my song;
And if you find it wondrous short,
    It cannot hold you long.

In Islington there was a man,                              5
    Of whom the world might say,
That still a godly race he ran
    When'er he went to pray.

A kind and gentle heart he had,
    To comfort friends and foes;                           10
The naked every day he clad,
    When he put on his clothes.

And in that town a dog was found,
    As many dogs there be,
Both mongrel, puppy, whelp, and hound,                     15
    And curs of low degree.

This dog and man at first were friends;
    But when a pique began,
The dog, to gain his private ends,
    Went mad, and bit the man.                             20

Around from all the neighbouring streets
    The wondering neighbours ran,
And swore the dog had lost his wits,
    To bite so good a man.

The wound it seemed both sore and sad                    25
   To every Christian eye:
And while they swore the dog was mad,
   They swore the man would die.

But soon a wonder came to light,
   That showed the rogues they lied;                30
The man recovered of the bite,
   The dog it was that died.

OLIVER GOLDSMITH (1728-1774)


## MORE LIMERICKS

She frowned and called him Mr.
Because in sport he kr.
    And so in spite
    That very night
This Mr. kr. sr.

\* \* \*

A diner while dining at Crewe
Found quite a large mouse in his stew.
    Said the waiter, "Don't shout
    And wave it about,
Or the rest will be wanting one, too."

\* \* \*

There was a young lady of Lynn,
    Who was so excessively thin,
    That when she assayed
    To drink lemonade
She slipped through the straw and fell in.

\* \* \*

A maiden at college, Miss Breeze,
Had B.A.'s and M.A.'s and Lit. D.'s.
    Said her doctor, "It's plain
    You'll collapse from the strain,
For you're killing yourself by degrees."

## DO THE PANTHERS
## PLAY THE BLUES
## FOR STEPHANIE

the harley is
painted silver
and the red saddle
is studded with
chrome tacks                                    5

it carries a
california license
plate and a red
and white flag

his afro                                        10
is bleached
and the tattoos
on his arms
and hands are
day-glo red                                     15

on the street
he/s easy to
follow as he
sells heroin
in weighted                                     20
foil pouches

and when i scoop
him he yells "you
can/t hold me i/m
american" and when                              25
i book him he asks
"how much is bail"
and pulls out his
plastic american
express card

HANS JEWINSKI (b. 1946)


## TRACKS

he told her it was like nothing she had ever felt before
he told her everybody was using it
he told her there was nothing to be afraid of
he told her nobody would know

he told her they would look like freckles anyway          5
he told her everything would be all right
he told her
and he told her
and he told her they were broke
and he told her nothing else would ease the pain          10
and he told her how to earn the money
and he told her nobody would know
and he told her everything would be all right
and you tell me that she/d been a mixed-up kid
and you tell me that you/d known right from the start     15
and you tell me that you/re clean
and you show me your smooth arms
and you tell me i/ve got nothing on you
and you tell me everybody knows
and you tell me everything will be all right              20
and i tell you you had better make tracks
or i/ll kill you

HANS JEWINSKI (b. 1946)


## THE TITANIC

The first 56 lines of the poem describe the christening of the
Titanic at the Harland and Wolff Works in Belfast on May 31,
1911, and its completion on March 31, 1912. She is the largest
ship on the ocean, one of the fastest, and is equipped with all the
latest safety devices such as wireless radio. Although she carries
only one-third the required number of lifeboats, no one is
worried because she is unsinkable. She is completed amidst
great publicity and is widely regarded as "the perfect ship."

THE ICEBERG

Calved from a glacier near Godhaven coast,
It left the fiord for the sea—a host
Of white flotillas gathering in its wake,
And joined by fragments from the Behring floe,     60
Had circumnavigated it to make
It centre of an archipelago.
Its lateral motion on the Davis Strait
Was casual and indeterminate,
And each advance to southward was as blind
As each recession to the north. No smoke
Of steamships nor the hoist of mainsails broke

The polar wastes—no sounds except the grind
Of ice, the cry of curlews and the lore
Of winds from mesas of eternal snow;                    70
Until caught by the western undertow,
It struck the current of the Labrador
Which swung it to its definite southern stride.
Pressure and glacial time had stratified
The berg to the consistency of flint,
And kept inviolate, through clash of tide
And gale, façade and columns with their hint
Of inward altars and of steepled bells
Ringing the passage of the parallels.
But when with months of voyaging it came           80
To where both streams—the Gulf and Polar—met,
The sun which left its crystal peaks aflame
In the sub-arctic noons, began to fret
The arches, flute the spires and deform
The features, till the batteries of storm,
Playing above the slow-eroding base,
Demolished the last temple touch of grace.
Another month, and nothing but the brute
And palaeolithic outline of a face
Fronted the transatlantic shipping route.           90
A sloping spur that tapered to a claw
And lying twenty feet below had made
It lurch and shamble like a plantigrade;
But with an impulse governed by the raw
Mechanics of its birth, it drifted where
Ambushed, fog-grey, it stumbled on its lair,
North forty-one degrees and forty-four,
Fifty and fourteen west the longitude,
Waiting a world-memorial hour, its rude
Corundum form stripped to its Greenland core.

SOUTHAMPTON, WEDNESDAY, APRIL 10, 1912

An omen struck the thousands on the shore—
A double accident! And as the ship
Swung down the river on her maiden trip,
Old sailors of the clipper decades, wise
To the sea's incantations, muttered fables
About careening vessels with their cables
Snapped in their harbours under peaceful skies.
Was it just suction or fatality
Which caused the *New York* at the dock to turn,
Her seven mooring ropes to break at the stern          110

And writhe like anacondas on the quay,
While tugs and fenders answered the collision
Signals with such trim margin of precision?
And was it backwash from the starboard screw
Which, tearing at the big *Teutonic*, drew
Her to the limit of her hawser strain,
And made the smaller tethered craft behave
Like frightened harbour ducks? And no one knew
For many days the reason to explain
The rise and wash of one inordinate wave,                    120
When a sunken barge on the Southampton bed
Was dragged through mire eight hundred yards ahead
As the *Titanic* passed above its grave.
But many of those sailors wise and old,
Who pondered on this weird mesmeric power,
Gathered together, lit their pipes and told
Of portents hidden in the natal hour,
Told of the launching of some square-rigged ships,
When water flowed from the inverted tips
Of a waning moon, of sun-hounds, of the shrieks          130
Of whirling shags around the mizzen peaks.
And was there not this morning's augury
For the big one now heading for the sea?
So long after she passed from landsmen's sight,
They watched her with their Mother Carey eyes
Through Spithead smoke, through mists of Isle of Wight
Through clouds of sea-gulls following with their cries.

Lines 138-268 describe the sumptuous meals and the luxurious
accommodations aboard the ship. In the gymnasium, professional wrestlers and instructors demonstrate their skills. The
passengers are calm and secure as the mighty engines power the
ship through the sea.

Throughout the day on Thursday, reports are received from
other ships warning of field ice in the area. All ships are warned
to slow down.

Three men talking on deck discuss the ice and are worried
about the ship's speed, but they have confidence in the captain
and in the watchfulness of the crew. They joke about a mummy
which the ship is carrying and which is supposed to bring death
to all who come in contact with it.

At dinner that evening, some of the wealthiest people in the
world discuss the ship's power, comfort and security. They have
great faith in the wireless radio, stating that if any accident did
occur other ships could be summoned and would arrive quickly.

Outside, the sky is clear and filled with stars. At 9:05 p.m. the
*Californian,* the closest ship to the *Titanic,* wires that she is
stopped because of the ice. Meanwhile, the carefree life on the
*Titanic* continues, as a poker game for high stakes is played.
At 11:45 p.m. the crow's nest watch sights an "iceberg dead!
On starboard bow!" These sections cover lines 269-676.

MURDOCH HOLDING THE BRIDGE-WATCH
     *Starboard your helm:* ship heeled
To port. From bridge to engine-room the clang
Of the telegraph. *Danger. Stop.* A hand sprang
To the throttle; the valves closed, and with the churn   680
Of the reverse the sea boiled at the stern.
Smith hurried to the bridge and Murdoch closed
The bulkheads of the ship as he supposed,
But could not know that with those riven floors
The electro-magnets failed upon the doors.
No shock! No more than if something alive
Had brushed her as she passed. The bow had missed.
Under the vast momentum of her drive
She went a mile. But why that ominous five
Degrees (within five minutes) of a list?     690

IN A CABIN:
*"What was that, steward?"*
     *"Seems like she hit a sea, sir."*
*"But there's no sea; calm as a landlocked bay*
*It is; lost a propeller blade?"*
     *"Maybe, sir."*
*"She's stopped."*
     *"Just cautious like, feeling her way,*
*There's ice about. It's dark, no moon to-night,*
*Nothing to fear, I'm sure, sir."*
     For so slight     700
The answer of the helm, it did not break
The sleep of hundreds: some who were awake
Went up on deck, but soon were satisfied
That nothing in the shape of wind or tide
Or rock or ice could harm the huge bulk spread
On the Atlantic, and went back to bed.

CAPTAIN IN WIRELESS ROOM:
*"We've struck an iceberg—glancing blow: as yet*
*Don't know extent; looks serious; so get*
*Ready to send out general call for aid;*    710
*I'll tell you when—having inspection made."*

REPORT OF SHIP'S CARPENTER AND FOURTH OFFICER:
A starboard cut three hundred feet or more
From foremast to amidships. Iceberg tore
Right at the bilge turn through the double skin:
Some boiler rooms and bunkers driven in;
The forward five compartments flooded—mail
Bags floating. Would the engine power avail
To stem the rush?

WIRELESS ROOM, FIRST OFFICER PHILLIPS AT KEY:
                                    *Titanic, C.Q.D.*                    720
*Collision: iceberg: damaged starboard side:*
*Distinct list forward.* (Had Smith Magnified
The danger? Over-anxious certainly.)
The second (joking)—*"Try new call, maybe*
*Last chance you'll have to send it."*

                                                    *S.O.S.*
Then back to older signal of distress.

On the same instant the *Carpathia* called,
The distance sixty miles—*Putting about,*
*And heading for you; Double watch installed*
*In engine room, in stokehold and look-out.*                    730
*Four hours the run, should not the ice retard*
*the speed; but taking chances: Coming hard!*

THE BRIDGE

As leaning on her side to ease a pain,
The tilted ship had stopped the captain's breath:
The inconceivable had stabbed his brain,
This thing unfelt—her visceral wound of death?
Another message—this time to report her
Filling, taxing the pumps beyond their strain.
Had that blow rent her from the bow to quarter?
Or would the aft compartments still intact                    740
Give buoyancy enough to counteract
The open forward holds?
                              The carpenter's
Second report had offered little chance,
And panic—heart of God—the passengers,
The fourteen hundred—seven hundred packed
In steerage—seven hundred immigrants!
Smith thought of panic clutching at their throats.
And feared that Balkan scramble for the boats.

No call from bridge, no whistle, no alarm

Was sounded. Have the stewards quietly                    750
Inform the passengers: no vital harm,
Precautions merely for emergency;
Collision? Yes, but nature of the blow
Must not be told: not even the crew must know:
Yet all on deck with lifebelts, and boats ready,
The sailors at the falls, and all hands steady.

In the wireless room, messages are received from ships in the
area, but the *Californian* is silent. The Titanic's best hope for
contact now is the *Carpathia*.

On the decks some people prepare to leave the ship, but most
of them are so sure of The Titanic's safety that they think this is
a useless exercise and are somewhat annoyed. In orderly fashion
they board the lifeboats and are surprised to see three red flares
fired off—a sign that the ship is in serious trouble.

The first lifeboat goes over the side as the midnight darkness
is lighted by the eerie glow of the icebergs.

The Carpathia radios that she is coming with all possible
speed.

The band plays, trying to keep the passengers calm as lifeboats, less than half-filled, are lowered. Many of the passengers
still aboard make jokes about those in the boats. Below decks,
the engineers work desperately to keep the ship's power up.
Meanwhile the captain of the *Carpathia* dangerously forces his
ship at full speed through the ice field. These passages cover
lines 757-951.

As yet no panic, but none might foretell
The moment when the sight of that oblique
Breath taking lift of the taffrail and the sleek
And foamless undulation of the swell
Might break in meaning on those diverse races,
And give them common language. As the throng
Came to the upper decks and moved along
The incline, the contagion struck the faces
With every lowering of a boat and backed            960
Them towards the stern. And twice between the hush
Of fear and utterance the gamut cracked,
When with the call for women and the flare
Of an exploding rocket, a short rush
Was made for the boats—fifteen and two.
'Twas nearly done—the sudden clutch and tear
Of canvas, a flurry of fists and curses met
By swift decisive action from the crew,

Supported by a quartermaster's threat
Of three revolver shots fired on the air.                          970

But still the fifteenth went with five inside,
Who, seeking out the shadows, climbed aboard
And, lying prone and still, managed to hide
Under the thwarts long after she was lowered.
*Jingle all the way,*
*O what fun....*

*"Some men in number two, sir!"*
                                        The boat swung
Back.
        *"Chuck the fellows out."*
                                        Grabbed by the feet,
The lot were pulled over the gunwale and flung        980
Upon the deck.
                *"Hard at that forward cleat!*
*A hand there for that after fall. Lower*
*Away—port side, the second hatch, and wait."*

With six hands of his watch, the bosun's mate,
Sent down to open up the gangway door,
Was trapped and lost in a flooded alley way,
And like the seventh, impatient of delay,
The second left with room for twenty more.

The fiddley leading from a boiler room
Lay like a tortuous exit from a tomb.                          990

A stoker climbed it, feeling by the twist
From vertical how steep must be the list.
He reached the main deck where the cold night airs
Enswathed his flesh with steam. Taking the stairs,
He heard the babel by the davits, faced
The forward, noticed how the waters raced
To the break of the fo'c'sle and lapped
The foremast root. He climbed again and saw
The resolute manner in which Murdoch's rapped
Command put a herd instinct under law;                        1000
No life-preserver on, he stealthily
Watched Phillips in his room, bent at the key,
And thinking him alone, he sprang to tear
The jacket off. He leaped too soon. *"Take that!"*
The second stove him with a wrench. *"Lie there,*
*Till hell begins to singe your lids—you rat!"*

But set against those scenes where order failed,

Was the fine muster at the fourteenth where,
Like a zone of calm along a thoroughfare,
The discipline of sea-worn laws prevailed.      1010
No women answering the repeated calls,
The men filled up the vacant seats: the falls
Were slipping through the sailors' hands,
When a steerage group of women, having fought
Their way over five flights of stairs, were brought
Bewildered to the rails. Without commands
Barked from the lips of officers; without
A protest registered in voice or face,
The boat was drawn up and the men stepped out
Back to the crowded stations with that free      1020
Barter of life for life done with the grace
And air of a Castilian courtesy.

*I've just got here through Paris,*
*From the sunny Southern shore,*
*I to Monte Carlo went....*
At the sixteenth—a woman wrapped her coat
Around her maid and placed her in the boat;
Was ordered in but seen to hesitate
At the gunwale, and more conscious of her pride
Than of her danger swiftly took her fate      1030
With open hands, and without show of tears
Returned unmurmuring to her husband's side;
*"We've been together now for forty years,*
*Whither you go, I go."*

                A boy of ten,
Ranking himself within the class of men,
Though given a seat, made up his mind to waive
The privilege of his youth and size, and piled
The inches on his stature as he gave
Place to a Magyar woman and her child.

And men who had in the world's run of trade,      1040
Or in pursuit of the professions, made
Their reputation, looked upon the scene
Merely as drama in a life's routine:
Millet was studying eyes as he would draw them
Upon a canvas; Butt, as though he saw them
In the ranks; Astor, social, debonair,
Waved *"Goodbye"* to his bride—*"See you to-morrow"*,
And tapped a cigarette on a silver case;
Men came to Guggenheim as he stood there

In evening suit, coming this time to borrow                    1050
Nothing but courage from his calm, cool face.

And others unobserved, of unknown name
And race, just stood behind, pressing no claim
Upon priority but rendering proof
Of their oblation, quiet and aloof
Within the maelstrom towards the rails. And some
Wavered a moment with the panic urge,
But rallied to attention on the verge
Of flight as if the rattle of a drum
From quarters faint but unmistakable                           1060
Had put the stiffening in the blood to check
The impulse of the feet, leaving the will
No choice between the lifeboats and the deck.

The four callapsibles, their lashings ripped,
Half-dragged, half-lifted by the hooks, were slipped
Over the side. The first two luckily
Had but the forward distance to the sea.
Its canvas edges crumpled up, the third
Began to fill with water and transferred
Its cargo to the twelfth, while number four,                   1070
Abaft and higher, nose-dived and swamped its score.

The wireless cabin—Phillips in his place,
Guessing the knots of the Cunarder's race.
Water was swirling up the slanted floor
Around the chair and sucking at his feet.
*Carpathia*'s call—the last one heard complete—
*Expect to reach position half-past four.*
The operators turned—Smith at the door
With drawn incredulous face. *"Men, you have done
Your duty. I release you. Everyone*                             1080
*Now for himself."* They stayed ten minutes yet,
The power growing fainter with each blue
Crackle of flame. Another stammering jet—
*Virginian* heard "a tattering C.Q.".
Again a try for contact but the code's
Last jest had died between the electrodes.

Even yet the spell was on the ship: although
The last lifeboat had vanished, there was no
Besieging of the heavens with a crescendo
Of fears passing through terror into riot—                     1090
But on all lips the strange narcotic quiet
Of an unruffled ocean's innuendo.

In spite of her deformity of line,
Emergent like a crag out of the sea,
She had the semblance of stability,
Moment by moment furnishing no sign,
So far as visible, of that decline
Made up of inches crawling into feet.
Then, with the electric circuit still complete,
The miracle of day displacing night                        1110
Had worked its fascination to beguile
Direction of the hours and cheat the sight.
Inside the recreation rooms the gold
From Arab lamps shone on the burnished tile.
What hindered the return to shelter while
The ship clothed in that irony of light
Offered her berths and cabins as a fold?
And, was there not the *Californian?*
Many had seen her smoke just over there,
But two hours past—it seemed a harbour span—              1120
So big, so close, she could be hailed, they said;
She must have heard the signals, seen the flare
Of those white stars and changed at once her course.
There under the *Titanic's* foremast head,
A lamp from the look-out cage was flashing Morse.
No ship afloat unless deaf, blind and dumb
To those three sets of signals but would come.
And when the whiz of a rocket bade men turn
Their faces to each other in concern
At shattering facts upon the deck, they found           1130
Their hearts take reassurance with the sound
Of the violins from the gymnasium, where
The bandsmen in their blithe insouciance
Discharged the sudden tension of the air
With the fox-trot's sublime irrelevance.

The fo'c'sle had gone under the creep
Of the water. Though without a wind, a lop
Was forming on the wells now fathoms deep.
The seventy feet—the boat deck's normal drop—
Was down to ten. Rising, falling, and waiting,
Rising again, the swell that edged and curled
Around the second bridge, over the top
Of the air-shafts, backed, resurged and whirled
Into the stokehold through the fiddley grating.

Under the final strain the two wire guys
Of the forward funnel tugged and broke at the eyes:

With buckled plates the stack leaned, fell and smashed
The starboard wing of the flying bridge, went through
The lower, then tilting at the davits crashed
Over, driving a wave aboard that drew                        1150
Back to the sea some fifty sailors and
The captain with the last of the bridge command.

Out on the water was the same display
Of fear and self-control as on the deck—
Challenge and hesitation and delay,
The quick return, the will to save, the race
Of snapping oars to put the realm of space
Between the half-filled lifeboats and the wreck.
The swimmers whom the waters did not take
With their instant death-chill struck out for the wake       1160
Of the nearer boats, gained on them, hailed
The steersmen and were saved: the weaker failed
And fagged and sank. A man clutched at the rim
Of a gunwale, and a woman's jewelled fist
Struck at his face: two others seized his wrist,
As he released his hold, and gathering him
Over the side, they staunched the cut from the ring.
And there were many deeds envisaging
Volitions where self-preservation fought
Its red primordial struggle with the "ought",               1170
In those high moments when the gambler tossed
Upon the chance and uncomplaining lost.

Aboard the ship, whatever hope of dawn
Gleamed from the *Carpathia*'s riding lights was gone,
For every knot was matched by each degree
Of list. The stern was lifted bodily
When the bow had sunk three hundred feet, and set
Against the horizon stars in silhouette
Were the blade curves of the screws, hump of the rudder
The downward pull and after buoyancy                         1180
Held her a minute poised but for a shudder
That caught her frame as with the upward stroke
Of the sea a boiler or a bulkhead broke.

Climbing the ladders, gripping shroud and stay,
Storm-rail, ringbolt or fairlead, every place
That might befriend the clutch of hand or brace
Of foot, the fourteen hundred made their way
To the heights of the aft decks, crowding the inches
Around the docking bridge and cargo winches.

And now that last salt tonic which had kept                    1190
The valour of the heart alive—the bows
Of the immortal seven that had swept
The strings to outplay, outdie their orders, ceased.
Five minutes more, the angle had increased
From eighty on to ninety when the rows
Of deck and port-hole lights went out, flashed back
A brilliant second and again went black.
Another bulkhead crashed, then following

The passage of the engines as they tore
From their foundations, taking everything           1200
Clean through the bows from 'midships with a roar
Which drowned all cries upon the deck and shook
The watchers in the boats, the liner took
Her thousand fathoms journey to her grave.

*    *    *    *    *

And out there in the starlight, with no trace
Upon it of its deed but the last wave
From the *Titanic* fretting at its base,
Silent, composed, ringed by its icy broods,
The grey shape with the palaeolithic face
Was still the master of the longitudes.                        1210


## Notes

*Behring floe* (l.60): ice floe from the Behring Straits.

*archipelago* (l.62): a group of islands.

*mesas* (l.70): high table-lands.

*stratified* (l.75): formed into compact layers.

*façade and columns ... parallels* (l.75-l.77): in this description of the
iceberg, the author likens its form to a cathedral. The (imaginary) bells
of the steeple ring at the latitude points (parallels) in the journey south.

*Gulf and Polar* (l.81): two great oceanic currents—the Gulf is of warm
water; the Polar is of cold.

*paleolithic* (l.89): pertaining to the earlier part of the prehistoric stone age.

*plantigrade* (l.89): flat-footed animal such as the bear or wolverine.

*Corundum* (l.100): refers to a crystallized mineral, variously coloured; of
the ruby and sapphire family, but opaque.

*anacondas* (l.111): large snakes which crush their prey.

*fenders* (l.112): wood or cable bumpers to protect a ship from damage.

*starboard screw* (l.114): the right-hand propeller.

*hawser strain* (l.116): strength of the mooring cable.

*mesmeric* (l.125): hypnotic.

*portent* (l.127): omen, sign.

*natal hour* (l.127): hour of birth.

*whirly shags . . . mizzen peaks* (l.131): cormorants (large birds) circling the mast heads of ships.

*augury* (l.132): omen, sign.

*Mother Carey eyes* (l.135): protective eyes; from *Mater Cara*, a name for the Virgin Mary who protects sailors.

*Spithead* (l.136): eastern part of the channel between the English county of Hampshire and the Isle of Wight.

*Starboard your helm* (l.677): turn the ship to starboard.

*list* (l.690): tilt, inclination to one side.

*a sea* (l.692): a wave, rough water.

*bilge turn* (l.715): the curved part of a ship's hull where its flat bottom and vertical sides are joined.

*C.Q.D.* (l.720): general call used at beginning of radiograms broadcasting general information.

*S.O.S.* (l.726): a wireless code signal of extreme distress.

*Putting about* (l.729): turning around.

*visceral wound* (l.736): wound to the internal organs.

*oblique breath . . . taffrail* (l.953-l.954): the taffrail is the flat area of the ship's stern. The author foretells the lifting of the stern as the Titanic begins to sink forward.

*gamut* (l.962): entire range; hence the author tells us that twice the passengers gradually raised their voices from a dead silence to a loud clamour.

*six hands of his watch* (l.985): six sailors on duty with him.

*fiddley* (l.989): uppermost part of the stokehole (or furnace) of a steam-ship.

*stove* (l.1005): delivered a crushing blow.

*muster* (l.1008): ordered assembly.

*steerage group* (l.1014): group of passengers travelling at the cheapest rate.

*Castilian courtesy* (l.1022): highly formalized courtesy of the Spanish nobility.

*Magyar* (l.1039): Hungarian.

*maelstrom* (l.1056): an extraordinarily large and violent whirlpool.

*collapsibles* (l.1064): collapsible rafts.

*narcotic quiet* (l.1091): drug-induced silence.

*blithe insouciance* (l.1133): cheerful indifference.

*lop* (1137): chop, as in choppy seas.

*wire guys* (1.1145): support wires.

*fagged* (1.1163): tired, became exhausted.

*deeds envisaging volitions . . . the "ought"* (1.1068-1.1070): acts which result from a struggle between the demands of morality and a desire for self-preservation.

*icy broods* (1.1208): smaller chunks of ice which broke off the main berg; its icy offspring.

# 4 POETS AND POEMS

---

## Introduction

"Sir, what is poetry?"
"Why, Sir, it is much easier to say what it is not. We all *know* what light is; but it is not easy to *tell* what it is."

SAMUEL JOHNSON

"What is jazz?"
"If you don't *know* what jazz is, there's no way I can explain it to you."

PROBABLY LOUIS ARMSTRONG

From your reading and discussions of poems, you have probably discovered that different people respond in different ways to poems. There has probably been a wide variety of interpretations for most poems in this collection. Because people respond so differently to poems, it is almost impossible to give a definition of poetry that will satisfy all poets or all readers of poetry.

Both the poet and the reader know that poetry is different from prose. Poetry looks different on the page; the language of poetry is usually different in some way; the effect or purpose of a poem is usually different from that of prose. In essence, a poem is an experience. Poets express their experiences, and readers try to achieve the same experiences by careful thought and examination of the poets' words.

Poetry is a special kind of communication. A simple model of the communication process is this:

S       ⟶       M       ⟶       R

sender            message            receiver

The poet is the sender; the poem is the message; the reader is the receiver. For poetry, the process might be drawn like this:

S       ⟶       M       ⟶       R

The poet's        The printed        The reader's

experience        verse            experience

The reader tries to achieve an experience as similar to that of the poet as possible. The reader searches for the sense of the words, the feeling, the tone and the intention.

We have seen some of the tools of the poet's craft such as imagery, rhythm and form. The reader must examine these and other features of the message. Both poet and reader must have some sensitivity to use devices to express a certain kind of message. The poet expects the reader to be thoughtful and sensitive to these devices to achieve the full meaning of the poem.

In summary, the reader expects the poet to give pleasure and meaning beyond the sense of the words. The reader expects the poem to point beyond the language itself. In turn, the poet expects the reader to enter into the poem openly and sensitively. The reader's experience must sometimes be set aside in order to enter into the poet's experience.

# Poems About Poetry

As you read these quotations see if you can find some common elements of poetry that several poets agree on.

- "Poetry—the best words in the best order."
  (Samuel Taylor Coleridge)
- "Poetry is the imaginative expression of strong feeling ... the spontaneous overflow of powerful feelings recollected in tranquillity."
  (William Wordsworth)
- "... speech framed ... to be heard for its own sake and interest even over and above its interest of meaning."
  (Gerard Manley Hopkins)

- "Poetry is language that tells us, through a more or less emotional reaction, something that cannot be said. All poetry, great or small, does this."

(Edwin Arlington Robinson)

We might choose three elements that characterize poetry and which make it different from prose.

- Content: what poetry is about
- Form: how poetry is designed
- Effect or Purpose: what poetry does

The content of poetry can be described in several ways. Poems are about emotion. The poet is moved by a scene or a thought or an experience of some kind to write a poem. This emotion is expressed in imaginative language. The poet chooses words that create pictures in the reader's mind to help the reader experience a similar emotion. The poet creates the poem because he or she believes that the experience is important or significant, that it will give us an insight into the human experience that we all share. Finally, the poet is sensitive to and writes about beauty in all its various forms. The content of poetry might be summarized as emotion expressed in imaginative language conveying a message of importance and beauty.

The second element of poetry is its form. The design of a poem as it is printed on the page shows that it is different from prose. More importantly, poems contain rhythm which is much more regular than that of prose. The delight of rhythm is in its relation to the meaning of the poem, in its uniformity and in its variations. The order of the words is a second feature of poetic form. Closed forms often demand a "poetic" arrangement of words and phrases. In open forms the poet carefully arranges words by themselves or in groups so that they will stand out for emphasis. Poems are also concise and compact and show an intense unity of thought and expression. That is, each word and phrase is rich in the four kinds of meaning° we have been discussing throughout this book. Finally, poems are concrete. The language of poems enables them to make abstract feelings concrete and substantial. The poet chooses specific words which are rich in connotation° and which suggest meanings by their sound and color as well as by their sense.

The third element of poetry is its purpose or effect. Poems carry a more sensual and emotional meaning than prose, and this meaning is conveyed in a more concise form.

Poems are the result of the inner compulsion of poets to express their experiences in a skillful manner. You, the reader, begin with this expression; and through your understanding of the craft and your ability to draw upon your own experiences, you recreate in your own mind a poet's experience.

## POETRY

Nothing can take its place. If I write "ostrich"
Those who have never seen the bird see it
With its head in the sand and its plumes fluffed with the
      wind
Like Mackenzie King talking on Freedom of Trade.

And if I write "holocaust," and "nightingales,"                              5
I startle the insurance agents and the virgins
Who belong, by this alchemy, in the same category,
Since both are very worried about their premiums.

A rose and a rose are two roses; a rose is a rose is a rose.
Sometimes I have walked down a street marked
      No Outlet                                                                            10
Only to find that what was blocking my path
Was a railroad track roaring away to the west.

So I know it will survive. Not even the decline of reading
And the substitution of advertising for genuine pornography
Can crush the uprush of the mushrooming verb
Or drown the overtone of the noun on its own.

F.R. SCOTT (b. 1899)


## Questions
1. What poetic devices has the poet used in the last two lines of the poem? For what effect do you think he used them?
2. What statement does the poem make about poetry?


## SONNET 55: NOT MARBLE NOR THE GILDED MONUMENTS

Not marble nor the gilded monuments
Of princes shall outlive this pow'rful rhyme;
But you shall shine more bright in these contents
Than unswept stone, besmear'd with sluttish time.
When wasteful war shall statues overturn,                                5
And broils root out the work of masonry,
Nor Mars his sword nor war's quick fire shall burn
The living record of your memory.

'Gainst death and all-oblivious enmity
Shall you pace forth; your praise shall still find room          10
Even in the eyes of all posterity,
That wear this world out to the ending doom.
   So, till the Judgment that yourself arise,
   You live in this, and dwell in lovers' eyes.

WILLIAM SHAKESPEARE (1564-1616)

## Notes

*rhyme* (l.2): poem.

*these contents* (l.3): what is contained in these sonnets (this is one of a
   series or sequence of sonnets).

*Than unswept stone . . . time* (l.4): than an unswept memorial stone dulled
   by time.

*wasteful* (l.5): laying waste, devastating.

*broils* (l.6): uprisings.

*nor* (l.7): neither.

*Mars his sword* (l.7): Mars' sword.

*all-oblivious enmity* (l.9): hostile to everything.

*Judgment that* (l.13): Judgment Day, when.

## Questions

1. What is the purpose of poetry as stated in this sonnet?
2. What characteristics of the sonnet form are present in this poem?


## TERENCE, THIS IS STUPID STUFF

   "Terence, this is stupid stuff:
You eat your victuals fast enough;
There can't be much amiss, 'tis clear,
To see the rate you drink your beer.
But oh, good Lord, the verse you make,          5
It gives a chap the belly-ache.
The cow, the old cow, she is dead;
It sleeps well, the horned head:
We poor lads, 'tis our turn now
To hear such tunes as killed the cow.          10
Pretty friendship 'tis to rhyme
Your friends to death before their time
Moping melancholy mad:
Come, pipe a tune to dance to, lad."

Why, if 'tis dancing you would be,        15
There's brisker pipes than poetry.
Say, for what were hop-yards meant,
Or why was Burton built on Trent?
Oh many a peer of England brews
Livelier liquor than the Muse,        20
And malt does more than Milton can
To justify God's ways to man.
Ale, man, ale's the stuff to drink
For fellows whom it hurts to think:
Look into the pewter pot        25
To see the world as the world's not.
And faith, 'tis pleasant till 'tis past:
The mischief is that 'twill not last.

Oh I have been to Ludlow fair
And left my necktie God knows where,        30
And carried half-way home, or near,
Pints and quarts of Ludlow beer:
Then the world seemed none so bad,
And I myself a sterling lad;
And down in lovely muck I've lain,        35
Happy till I woke again.
Then I saw the morning sky:
Heigho, the tale was all a lie;
The world, it was the old world yet,
I was I, my things were wet,        40
And nothing now remained to do
But begin the game anew.

Therefore, since the world has still
Much good, but much less good than ill,
And while the sun and moon endure        45
Luck's a chance, but trouble's sure,
I'd face it as a wise man would,
And train for ill and not for good.
'Tis true, the stuff I bring for sale
Is not so brisk a brew as ale:        50
Out of a stem that scored the hand
I wrung it in a weary land.
But take it: if the smack is sour,
The better for the embittered hour;
It should do good to heart and head        55
When your soul is in my soul's stead;
And I will friend you, if I may,
In the dark and cloudy day.

There was a king reigned in the East:
There, when kings will sit to feast,                    60
They get their fill before they think
With poisoned meat and poisoned drink.
He gathered all that springs to birth
From the many-venomed earth;
First a little, thence to more,                         65
He sampled all her killing store;
And easy, smiling, seasoned sound,
Sate the king when healths went round.
They put arsenic in his meat
And stared aghast to watch him eat;                     70
They poured strychnine in his cup
And shook to see him drink it up:
They shook, they stared as white's their shirt:
Them it was their poison hurt.
—I tell the tale that I heard told.                     75
Mithridates, he died old.

A.E. HOUSMAN (1859-1936)

## Notes

*Terence, This is Stupid Stuff*: the original volume in which this poem
appeared was entitled, "The Poems of Terence Hearsay."

*Burton* (l.18): an English town famous for its ales.

*than Milton can* ... (l.22): In the opening of his great poem "Paradise
Lost," Milton said his purpose was to "justify the ways of God to men."

*Ludlow fair* (l.29): the village fair would be the highlight of a youth's social
life.

*smack* (l.53): taste, flavor.

*I will friend you* (l.57): I will be your friend.

*Mithridates* (l.76): the ancient king of Pontus who developed a tolerance
for poison by taking gradually increasing amounts.

## Questions

1. Are the tone and intention of this poem serious or humorous? Support
   your opinion by references to the language and form.

## POETRY

I, too, dislike it: there are things that are important beyond all this
      fiddle.
Reading it, however, with a perfect contempt for it, one discovers in
it after all, a place for the genuine.
      Hands that can grasp, eyes
      that can dilate, hair that can rise                           5
        if it must, these things are important not because a

high-sounding interpretation can be put upon them but because they
      are
useful. When they become so derivative as to become unintelligible,
the same thing may be said for all of us, that we
      do not admire what                                 10
      we cannot understand: the bat
      holding on upside down or in quest of something to

eat, elephants pushing, a wild horse taking a roll, a tireless wolf under
a tree, the immovable critic twitching his skin like a horse that feels a
      flea, the base-
ball fan, the statistician—                                 15
      nor is it valid
      to discriminate against "business documents and

school-books"; all these phenomena are important. One must make a
      distinction
however: when dragged into prominence by half poets, the result
      is not poetry,
nor till the poets among us can be                         20
      "literalists of
      the imagination"—above
      insolence and triviality and can present

for inspection, "imaginary gardens with real toads in them," shall
      we have
it. In the meantime, if you demand on the one hand,            25
the raw material of poetry in
      all its rawness and
      that which is on the other hand
      genuine, you are interested in poetry.

MARIANNE MOORE (1887-1972)


## Questions

1. What value of poetry is suggested in the poem?
2. What criticisms are made of poor poetry?

## ARS POETICA

A poem should be palpable and mute
As a globed fruit,

Dumb
As old medallions to the thumb,

Silent as the sleeve-worn stone                                    5
Of casement ledges where the moss has grown—

A poem should be wordless
As the flight of birds.

A poem should be motionless in time
As the moon climbs,                                               10

Leaving, as the moon releases
Twig by twig the night-entangled trees,

Leaving, as the moon behind the winter leaves,
Memory by memory the mind—

A poem should be motionless in time                               15
As the moon climbs.

A poem should be equal to:
Not true.

For all the history of grief
An empty doorway and a maple leaf.                                20

For love
The leaning grasses and two lights above the sea—

A poem should not mean
But be.

ARCHIBALD MacLEISH (b. 1892)

**Notes**
*Ars Poetica*: Latin for "The Art of Poetry," the title of an essay on poetry
by the Roman poet Horace (65-8 B.C.).

**Question**
1. What does the poem mean?

## JOHNNIE'S POEM

Look! I've written a poem!
Johnnie says
and hands it to me
    and it's about
    his grandfather dying           5
    last summer, and me
    in the hospital
and I want to cry,
don't you see, because it doesn't matter
if it's not very good:           10
    what matters is he knows
and it was me, his father, who told him
    you write poems about what
    you feel deepest and hardest.

ALDEN NOWLAN (1933-1983)

### Questions

1. According to this poem, what is the purpose of poetry?
2. Describe the form of this poem.

# Poems for Interpretation

As you read these poems, try to apply what you have learned about the
language of poetry, poetic form and the different kinds of poems. Create
your own questions for study and discussion.

## SONG 61

    *What does poetry do*
*then?* he asked me
not having liked my poems,
not thinking them "poems" at all he said.

& what could i say to him i had           5
nothing to offer beyond
    (the poems)/

      & i have
no answer for you

no answer that would do                          10
    what you want it to, what
you want me to

        do, writing poems
    for you/for

what?        that you might say     15
    you like them/& who
        else.

All else failing      this answer:

*If possible, poetry sings.*
*Sings poetry, if possible.*                     20

no answer/no response
    in his eyes/i
could not be seen could not be
      heard?

i must still                                      25
      however
          sing.

DOUGLAS BARBOUR (b. 1940)

## ON THE VALUE OF FANTASIES

The teacher on the morning radio program
disapproves because her girl students
have such unrealistic fantasies.
They all think they will go to college,
marry a lawyer or a professor,                    5
have two kids and two cars,
and live happily ever after.

And she gets them to play a game
in which Linda becomes a widow at fifty,
Paulette is deserted at thirty-five             10
and has to bring up four kids
on a steno's salary, and poor Jennifer
never marries at all.
How will they cope?

Of course it's a matter of                        15
one fantasy against another;
and sometimes it's fun
to imagine oneself bearing up against adversity.

Myself, though, I agree with the kids
that it's rather a dumb game.                                    20
It's true, life is full of these dirty tricks,
but being prepared for the worst may make it happen.

(More might be said
for fantasizing about space travel
or maybe about being a mermaid.)                                 25

I still hope (two months before my fifty-third birthday)
that I may yet meet that handsome stranger
all the fortunetellers have told me about;
that sometime my lottery ticket
will win a tax-free fortune,                                     30
and that my poems become household words
and make the next edition of Columbo's *Quotations.*

I might as well believe in heaven, too,
for all the good it will do me to admit
statistics are against it.                                       35

ELIZABETH BREWSTER (b. 1922)


## THE FUTURE OF POETRY IN CANADA

Some people say we live in a modern mechanized nation
where the only places that matter
are Toronto, Montreal, and maybe Vancouver;
but I myself prefer Goodridge, Alberta,
a town where electricity arrived in 1953,                        5
the telephone in 1963.

In Goodridge, Alberta
the most important social events
have been the golden wedding anniversaries of the residents.
There have been a Garden Club, a Junior Grain Club, and a
    Credit Union.                                                10
and there have been farewell parties,
well attended in spite of the blizzards.

Weather is important in Goodridge.
People remember the time they threshed in the snow,
and the winter the temperature fell to seventy below.           15

They also remember the time
the teacher from White Rat School
piled eight children in his car
and drove them, as a treat,

all the way to Edmonton;           20
where they admired the Jubilee Auditorium
and the Parliament Buildings
and visited the CNR wash rooms
but were especially thrilled
going up and down in an elevator.        25

I hope at least one poet
in the next generation
comes from Goodridge, Alberta.

ELIZABETH BREWSTER (b. 1922)


## ON THE OTHER SIDE OF THE POEM

On the other side of the poem there is an orchard,
and in the orchard, a house with a roof of straw,
and three pine trees,
three watchmen who never speak, standing guard.

On the other side of the poem there is a bird,     5
yellow brown with a red breast,
and every winter he returns
and hangs like a bud in the naked bush.

On the other side of the poem there is a path
as thin as a hairline cut,               10
and someone lost in time
is treading the path barefoot, without a sound.

On the other side of the poem amazing things may happen,
even on this overcast day,
this wounded hour                 15
that breathes its fevered longing in the window pane.

On the other side of the poem my mother may appear
and stand in the doorway for a while lost in thought
and then call me home as she used to call me home long ago:
You've played enough, Rachel. Don't you see it's night?    20

RACHEL KORN (1898-1982)


## THE BIRD

The bird you captured is dead.
I told you it would die
but you would not learn

from my telling. You wanted
to cage a bird in your hands                                    5
and learn to fly.

Listen again.
You must not handle birds.
They cannot fly through your fingers.
You are not a nest                                            10
and a feather is
not made of blood and bone.

Only words
can fly for you like birds
on the wall of the sun.                                        15
A bird is a poem
that talks of the end of cages.

PATRICK LANE (b. 1939)

# Glossary

**Alliteration:** the repetition of sounds in nearby words, usually involving the first consonant sounds of the words. Often used to reinforce meaning or to imitate a sound relevant to what is being described.
For example: fair freedom's flag; the murmuring of innumerable bees.

**Allusion:** a reference to a famous literary, mythological, Biblical, or historical figure or event.
For example: He met his *Waterloo*; *Cupid's* arrows struck them.
An allusion adds to the depth of meaning of a poem since it reminds the reader of an entire story which can be applied to the poem.

**Anapestic:** a metrical foot made up of three syllables: two unstressed followed by one stressed (*υυ/*). It is often used in light-hearted or humorous poems.
For example: like a ghost; 'Twas the night before Christmas and all through the house.

**Apostrophe:** directly addressing an abstract quality or a nonexistent person as though it were present; therefore, a form of personification.
For example: O Canada; Death, where is thy sting?
Often used in patriotic poetry and to express some deep emotion. Also used to satirize or parody such poems.

**Assonance:** the repetition of vowel sounds in a line or series of lines of poetry.
For example:
Our echoes roll from soul to soul
And grow for ever and ever.
Often used to slow the pace of a poem; that is, the speed at which the reader reads it.

**Ballad:** a narrative poem, usually containing much repetition and often a repeated refrain.
Ballads were originally folk songs passed on from age to age. Ballads often tell of a single dramatic episode such as the sinking of a ship or a fight over a beautiful woman.

For example: see *Frankie and Johnny* (p. 179).

**Blank Verse:** a form of verse which is written in iambic pentameter and is not rhymed. Most of Shakespeare's plays are in blank verse because it can be used to imitate normal speech patterns in English.
For example: see *Ulysses* (p. 51).

**Caesura:** a significant pause within a line of poetry. Used to make the reader consider an idea or to show a transition in thought. Usually, but not always, occurs at a punctuation mark, but sometimes after a phrase or clause or after an internal rhyme. Shown in scansion by a double slash (//), as opposed to the single slash (/) which shows the end of a foot.
For example: Cover her
   face://mine eyes
   dazzle://she died young.
And priests in black
gowns//were walking their
rounds.

**Closed Form:** a poem written in a set pattern.
For example, the sonnet or the ode, which makes certain demands on the poet regarding structure, metre, rhyme scheme, and sometimes, imagery. Most older poetry is in closed form.

**Connotation:** the feelings and associations suggested by a word.
For example: note the different associations of the words horse; steed; nag.
Skillful use of connotations enables the poet to suggest wide-ranging attitudes for certain words. Connotations play a vital role in setting the feeling and tone of a poem.

**Dactylic:** a metrical foot made up of three syllables: the first one stressed, the next two unstressed ( /∪∪ ).
For example: Lázily; Táke her úp ténderly.
Often used in comic verse or as a variation from the basic metre of the poem.

**Denotation:** the literal meaning or dictionary meaning of a word.
For example: horse—a large, four-legged animal with solid hoofs and a mane and tail of long, coarse hair.
Note that many common English words have several denotations and can be used as more than one part of speech—e.g. a run, run home, a run counter.

**Didactic:** a form of poem which has as its primary intention the teaching of some lesson or moral or the making of some critical statement about society.

An example of a didactic poem is *A Poison Tree* (p. 191).

**Double Rhyme:** a rhyme of two or more syllables in which rhyming stressed syllables are followed by rhyming unstressed syllables.
For example: fállinğ—cállinğ; sín̆g tŏ hĕr—clín̆g tŏ hĕr.
Often used for comic effect—e.g. platinum—flatten 'em, but occasionally used in serious verse. Also called feminine rhyme.

**Dramatic Monologue:** a lyric poem in which the speaker addresses his or her words to someone who is present but silent. The speaker becomes a character in a dramatic situation and his or her words, which are spoken at a decisive or revealing moment, give some insight into the speaker, perhaps unwittingly.
An example of a dramatic monologue is *Dover Beach* (p. 79).

**Elegy:** a formal poem, often written as a lament for a departed friend or respected person. The poet usually sets forth his or her ideas about death or some other serious subject.
An example of an elegy is *Elegy Written in a Country Churchyard* (p. 188).
Because of the serious nature of elegies, they are often paradied or satirized—e.g. *An Elegy on the Death of a Mad Dog* (p. 207).

**End-Stopped Line:** a full pause at the end of a line of poetry, usually marked by a punctuation mark.
For example:
> True wit is nature to advantage dressed,
> What oft was thought, but ne'er so well expressed.

The opposite of a run-on line.

**Epic:** a long narrative poem which tells of the adventures of heroic characters, covers a long period of time, or describes some monumental task. Often, supernatural forces play a part in the action.
An example of an epic is *The Titanic* (p. 210)
Because epics are often written in elaborate, elevated language, they are frequently parodied, though the parodies are generally much shorter than the originals.

**Epigram:** a short, concise poem which summarizes some valuable truth. Usually the poem leads up to a sudden twist or witty turn of thought in the last line. Though often humorous, some epigrams are serious. The form is used to make the statement or theme easily memorable.
An example of an epigram is *Outwitted* (p. 55).

**Exact Rhyme:** a rhyme in which the sounds after the vowel sounds are the same. For example: dead—head; slavery—knavery See also slant rhyme.

**End rhyme:** rhyme which comes at the end of lines. Most rhyme in poetry is end rhyme. See also internal rhyme.

**Feeling:** one of the four kinds of meaning; how the speaker of the words of the poem feels about what he or she is discussing.

**Figurative Language:** variations from the normal order, structure, or meaning of words to gain strength and depth of expression or to create a visual or other sensory effect in the reader's mind. Examples of figurative language are simile, metaphor, and personification. See also literal meaning.

**Figures of Speech:** the various techniques or devices of figurative language. Thus simile, metaphor and personification are examples of figures of speech.

**Foot:** a unit of rhythm within a line of poetry. A foot is usually made up of a stressed syllable and one or more unstressed syllables. For example: U/ is an iambic foot; /UU is a dactylic foot.

The number of feet in a line is used when describing metre. The pentametre is a five-foot line, the hexametre is a six-foot line, etc. See also p. 157 and *Metrical Feet* (p. 158).

**Form:** the pattern or structure or organization of a poem; the design of the poem as a whole. Two common poetic forms are the sonnet and the epigram. See also closed form and open form.

**Iambic:** a metrical foot made up of one unstressed syllable followed by one stressed syllable (U/). For example: Along/the line/of smok/y hills. This is the most common metrical foot in English is poetry.

**Image:** in poetry, a word or sequence of words that refers to a sensory experience. Images may be stated in either figurative language (e.g. The wind roared and struck her as she walked.) or in literal language (e.g. I saw a field of white daisies swaying in the breeze.). Imagery, then, is not a synonym for figurative language. An image always appeals to one or more of the senses.

Imagery, in its broad sense, means the pattern or collection of images within a poem or other literary work.

**Imagery:** the collection or pattern of images within a poem or other artistic work. A study of the imagery of a poem could either be of the physical world presented through the poem or of the devices (figures of speech) which the poet used.

**Intention:** one of the four kinds of meaning; the poet's apparent purpose in writing the poem or in expressing the ideas presented in it.

**Internal Rhyme:** rhyme which occurs within lines of poetry. For example:

> Now Sam McGee was from Tennessee where the cotton blooms and blows.

Often used to give strength and vigor to a poem since it seems to make the action occur more rapidly.

**Irony:** in poetry, a difference which the reader senses between the words that are spoken and what is true. Some techniques used to achieve irony are overstatement, understatement, and outright contradiction.

**Limerick:** a humorous, five-line poem, usually in anapestic rhythm; the first, second, and fifth lines have three feet and rhyme with each other; the third and fourth lines have two feet and rhyme with each other. Limericks usually tell of the actions of a person.

**Literal Meaning:** the exact meaning of a word or phrase taken without any added exaggeration, imagination, or connotations. Literal meaning, then, is similar to denotation. Literal language is the opposite of figurative language

**Lyric:** a short poem expressing the internal and emotional thoughts of a single speaker. Lyrics are usually an expression of the poet's feelings about a person, an object, an event or an idea. The intent is usually to create a single, unified impression on the reader. Lyrics originated as songs, and they retain their melodic patterns through various forms of rhythm and rhyme.

**Meaning:** four aspects of meaning may be considered: (1) the sense—what the poem is trying to communicate; (2) the feeling—the attitude of the speaker or poet to the subject; (3) the tone—the attitude of the speaker or poet to the reader or audience; (4) the intention—the effect or purpose the poem seems to be trying to achieve. Meanings of words can also be considered as denotation or connotation. The meaning of a poem might also be considered as the statement the poem makes and the emotions it evokes about the subject.

**Metaphor:** a form of figurative language which makes a comparison by stating that two items are the same—that one is the other.
For example:
> He was a roaring lion.
> They were falcons in a snare.

Metaphors may be called *extended metaphors* when they are especially drawn out or when they are central to the organization of the poem.
Metaphors may be *implied* when the quality of one item is applied to another although the two are not stated.
For example: He flew to her rescue. (He is given the quality of a bird although a bird is not mentioned.)
Metaphors are used to enrich the connotations of words and to state concisely a variety of meanings. To say a person is a star does not require one to list all the qualities of an actual star.

**Metre:** the pattern of stressed syllables which occurs at regular intervals and makes up the rhythm of a verse.
See also foot, iambic, anapestic, dactylic, and spondaic.

**Mood:** the attitude or tone which runs through an entire poem; the attitude which the poet takes toward the subject and theme.

Often used with the same meaning as tone.
See also tone.

**Narrative:** a poem that tells a story and organizes its action according to a sequence of time (though not necessarily in chronological order).

**Ode:** a poem on an exalted theme, expressed in dignified, sincere language, serious in tone, and usually in praise of something or somebody.
Because of their serious nature, odes are often parodied or satirized.

**Open Form:** a poem which follows no set pattern of rhyme or rhythm. The poet uses white space and varying line lengths to achieve emphasis. Most modern poetry is in open form. Sometimes called "free verse". See also closed form.

**Overstatement:** a figure of speech in which an exaggerated statement is made.
For example: My feet are killing me.
Also called hyperbole. May be used in both serious and humorous verse. Often used in love poems.

**Paraphrase:** a statement in prose which states the same thing as a given poem, though in different words. That is, putting into one's own words what one understands the poem is saying. Usually, the first step in interpreting a poem is to write a paraphrase of it or of the difficult passages in it.

**Pardoy:** a poem written in humorous imitation of another poem. Usually, the parody imitates the tone, form and imagery of the original, but applies them to some ridiculous object.

**Personification:** a figure of speech in which a non-human thing is given human attributes.
For example: beauty, honor, death, flowers have all been described as having human emotions or other human characteristics. Flowers may be said to dance in the wind. Death may be said to reach out to someone. Similar in some uses to apostrophe.

**Poem:** It is not possible to give a definition of a poem that will satisfy all readers. A poem may be described as a composition written for the purpose of giving artistic or emotional pleasure and characterized as having imagination, emotion, truth, sense impressions, concrete language and significant meaning, and being expressed in rhythmic language.

**Purpose:** the poet's or speaker's apparent reason for expressing the ideas contained in the poem. See also intention.

**Pyrrhic:** a metric foot made up of two unstressed syllables ($\cup\cup$). Rarely found in English poetry.

**Rhyme:** similarity of vowel sound and all sounds after the vowel in the relevant words. Rhyme is used to give a pleasing sound to a poem, to establish the form of a poem or stanza, and to unify and separate the divisions of a poem. Much modern poetry does not contain rhyme.

**Rhyme Scheme:** the pattern of rhyme within a stanza or poem. The rhyme scheme is usually shown by applying to each similar rhyme the same letter of the alphabet.
For example:

```
... steeple        a
... town           b
... people         a
... down           b
```

**Rhythm:** in poetry, the pattern of stressed and unstressed sounds in a poem. All spoken language has rhythm; however, it is not as regular as the rhythm of poetry. Rhythm in poetry is analysed by scansion.

**Run-On Line:** the carrying over of sense and grammatical

structure from one line of poetry to the following line; sometimes from one stanza to the next. Used to affect the rhythm of the poem by causing pauses to fall within lines rather than at the ends.
For example:

> At 12, instructed
> by the comic books already
> latent in my head . . .

Also called enjambement. See also end-stopped line.

**Satire:** a humorous criticism of a person or persons, or of some aspect of human behavior, or of some human institution or creation. A form of didactic poetry.

**Scansion:** the analysis of the patterns of stress within a poem. A way to listen to the sound of a poem to hear its effects. Scansion indicates the basic metre of a poem and the variations in it. Often these variations are related to important aspects of meaning, so scansion can also be an aid to interpretation.

**Sense:** the literal meaning of the poem; one of the four aspects of meaning (along with feeling, tone, intention). The sense of a poem can often be stated in a paraphrase.

**Simile:** a figure of speech in which there is a direct statement of the similarity between two items, usually through the use of a word such as *like*, *as*, or *than*, or by a verb such as *resembles*.
For example: My love is like a red, red rose.
Note that the two things being compared are essentially dissimilar. It is not a simile to say, "My car is like your car." See also metaphor.

**Single Rhyme:** a rhyme of one-syllable words or, in words of more than one syllable, a rhyme of stressed final syllables.
For example: fun—run; annoy—employ.
Also called masculine rhyme.

**Slack Syllable:** an unstressed syllable. Slack syllables may be used to gain an effect of hesitation or uncertainty, but when used in pairs as in the anapestic foot (∪∪/) they can give a bouncing rollicking rhythm.
For example: A bunch/of the boys/were whoop/ing it up/ in the Mal/amute/saloon.
Or, for a serious effect as in Poe's *Annabel Lee* (p. 68).

**Slant Rhyme:** A rhyme in which the words have similar but not exactly the same rhyming sounds, or in which the final consonants are the same but the vowels differ.
For example: black—rock; web—step; bend—wand.

When analysing rhyme the reader should consider if the apparent slant rhyme is the result of changes in pronunciation since the poem was written.
For example: say—tea was once an exact rhyme (say—tay).
Slant rhymes in modern poetry are probably intended as such.
Also called near rhyme, partial rhyme, and off rhyme.

**Sonnet:** a lyric poem of fourteen lines in iambic pentameter following one of several possible rhyme schemes. The two main types of sonnet are the Italian (or Petrarchan) and the English (or Shakespearean).
The Italian sonnet is divided into two parts: an eight-line section (octave) rhymed *abba abba*, and a six-line section (sestet) rhymed *cde cde* or *cdc cdc* or *cde cde*. Often the octave states a problem or a question and the sestet offers a solution.
The English sonnet usually has three four-line sections, each with its own rhyme scheme, and ends in a two-line rhymed couplet. The rhyme scheme, then, is usually *abab cdcd efef gg*. The final couplet is usually a concluding statement commenting on the preceding thoughts.
The sonnet is an example of closed form.

**Speaker:** the person or persons who speak the words of the poem. Poets often create a fictional character as playwrights do. The speaker must then speak in a certain way according to the situation presented in the poem. When the author is clearly speaking in his or her own terms, it is acceptable to speak of the poet rather than the speaker; but this is often hard to decide. Reading several poems by the same author may help a reader to see similarities in tone and feeling which might distinguish speaker from poet.
Also called the persona.

**Spondaic:** a metrical foot made up of two stressed syllables ($//$). Rare in English poetry and most likely to be found when two one-syllable words are used together.
For example: all jóy.
Also occurs in many compound words—e.g. football, heartbreak.
Used to give emphasis, to vary the basic emphasis and to vary the basic metre of the poem.

**Stanza:** a group of two or more lines in a poem linked on the basis of length, metre, rhyme scheme, or thought (more common in modern poetry). Each stanza is usually set off from the preceding and following stanzas by space. A traditional stanza form is the ballad. Strictly speaking, a stanza is not the same as a verse. See also verse.

**Structure:** in poetry, the way a poem is put together. Because poems are unified wholes, structure will be shown in patterns of various kinds within the poem. One kind of structure is syntactic—the sentences that make up the poem. Another kind of structure is the pattern of images that recur throughout the poem or at important points in it. A third kind of structure is found in the pattern of rhythm and/or rhyme. Other kinds of structure may also be found.
For example: a sonnet has fourteen lines divided into two groups, either 12 lines and 2, or 8 lines and 6. Narrative poems usually have a dramatic structure consisting of an introduction, conflict, rising action, climax and conclusion. Structure is most easily discovered through repeated and relatively fast readings of the entire poem. A sense of a poem's structure is an essential step towards more detailed interpretations.

**Symbol:** a term with many meanings; basically a symbol is something that stands for something else—e.g. a star, an ocean, a flag, a prison. Symbols depend on the connotations the reader attributes to them; hence they suggest or evoke meanings rather than state them directly.

**Theme:** in poetry, the central thought of the poem as a whole; the abstract concept which is made concrete through the imagery and other features of the poem. Theme is not the same as the subject or topic of the poem. It may be helpful to think of theme as the statement the poem makes about the topic. A one- or two-sentence paraphrase is a way of clarifying one's thoughts about the theme.

**Tone:** one of the four aspects of the meaning of a poem; the attitude the poet takes toward the audience. Thus, tone may be any of the normal human attitudes—e.g. angry, serious, mocking, humorous. The reader should be aware of the tone of a poem so that he or she may know the feelings he or she is to share while reading it.

**Topic:** the subject matter of a poem; also called the subject. For example: death, love, people, war.
Most poems make some statement about the topic. See also theme.

**Trochaic:** a metrical foot made up of two syllables: the first stressed, the second unstressed ($\prime\cup$).
For example:
Dóublĕ/dóublĕ/tóil ănd/tróublĕ./
Its most common use is in short songs and lyrics because in longer works the rhythm tends to be too repetitious.

**Understatement:** a figure of speech in which something is deliberately underrated or said to be less than it is.
Understatement has the effect of implying that the thing described is more than it is, allowing the reader to add the significance. Understatement is, therefore, a form of irony.
For example: upon winning a million dollar lottery, you say "That's nice."

**Unity:** the wholeness of a poem in which the entire poem is seen as being organized around a basic form or idea and to which all the parts are related. A poem has unity when the ideas, the form and the language all seem to contribute to presenting a single meaning or unifed impression.

**Verse:** used with two meanings: first, referring to a line of poetry; second, as a general name given to poetry (e.g. The Book of Modern Verse). Sometimes loosely used to refer to a stanza in poetry, though the two terms are better kept distinct.

# Index of Authors

# Index of Titles

# Acknowledgements

**Chronology** by Margaret Atwood. Reprinted from *The Animals in That Country* by Margaret Atwood © Oxford University Press.
**Greetings From the Incredible Shrinking Woman** by Pat Lowther. Reprinted from *A Stone Diary* by Pat Lowther © Oxford University Press.
**Our Daily Death** by Sid Marty. From *Nobody Danced With Miss Rodeo, Poems* by Sid Marty. Used by permission of The Canadian Publishers, McClelland and Stewart Limited, Toronto.
**My Brother Dying** is reprinted from *Collected Poems of Raymond Souster* by permission of Oberon Press.
**The Unknown Citizen** by W.H. Auden. Reprinted by permission of Faber and Faber Ltd. from *Collected Poems* by W.H. Auden.
**L'Envoi: in Beechwood Cemetery** by Harry Howith from *Multiple Choices: New and Selected Poems 1961-1976* (Oakville and Ottawa/Valley Editions 1977) by permission of the author.
**The Chance-Taking Dead** by R.G. Everson is reprinted from *Everson at 80* by permission of Oberon Press.
**First Person Demonstrative** by Phyllis Gotlieb. Reprinted by permission of the author.
**Love Under the Republicans (or Democrats)** by Ogden Nash. Copyright 1930 by Ogden Nash. First appeared in *The New Yorker.*
**Memory** by David Helwig is reprinted from *Figures in a Landscape* by permission of Oberon Press.
**Marriage** by Alden Nowlan. From *I'm a Stranger Here Myself* by Alden Nowlan © 1974 by Clarke, Irwin & Company Limited. Used by Permission of Irwin Publishing Inc.
**Someone Who Used To Have Someone** by Miriam Waddington. Reprinted from *The Price of Gold* by Miriam Waddington. © Miriam Waddington by permission of Oxford University Press.
**Acquainted with the Night** by Robert Frost. From *The Poetry of Robert Frost* edited by Edward Connery Lathem. Copyright 1923, 1928, © 1969 by Holt, Rinehart and Winston. Copyright 1951, © 1956 by Robert Frost. Reprinted by permission of Holt, Rinehart and Winston, Publishers.
**The Forsaken** by Duncan Campbell Scott. The work of Duncan Campbell Scott is reproduced with the permission of John G. Aylen, Ottawa, Canada.

257

bridge, Mass.: The Belknap Press of Harvard University Press, Copyright 1951, © 1955, 1979, 1983 by the President and Fellows of Harvard College.
**O Earth, Turn!** by George Johnston. Reprinted by permission; © 1955, 1983 The New Yorker Magazine, Inc.
**MacDonald's Camp** by Joe Townsend. Reprinted from *Lumbering Songs from the Northern Woods* by Edith Fowke.
**Canadian Railroad Trilogy** by Gordon Lightfoot, © 1967 Warner Bros. Inc. All Rights Reserved. Used by permission.
**Second Degree Burns** by Gwendolyn MacEwen is reprinted from *The Fire-Eaters* by permission of Oberon Press.
**The Crumbling Wall** by George Bowering. From *Touch: Selected Poems 1960-70* by George Bowering. Used by permission of The Canadian Publishers, McClelland and Stewart Limited, Toronto.
**Reflecting Sunglasses** by Pat Lowther. Reprint from *A Stone Diary* by Pat Lowther © Oxford University Press.
**Unemployment** by Tom Wayman. From *Waiting for Wayman* by Tom Wayman. Used by permission of The Canadian Publishers, McClelland and Stewart Limited, Toronto.
**Fire and Ice** by Robert Frost. From *The Poetry of Robert Frost* edited by Edward Connery Lathem. Copyright 1923, 1928, © 1969 by Holt, Rinehart and Winston. Copyright 1951, © 1956 by Robert Frost. Reprinted by permission of Holt, Rinehart and Winston, Publishers.
**Naming of Parts** by Henry Reed. Naming of Parts by Henry Reed from *A Map of Verona*. Reprinted by permission of Jonathan Cape Ltd., publisher.
**Can. Hist.** by Earle Birney. From *The Collected Poems of Earle Birney*. Used by permission of The Canadian Publishers, McClelland and Stewart Limited, Toronto.
**Dream Deferred** by Langston Hughes. Copyright 1951 by Langston Hughes. Reprinted from *The Panther and the Lash*, by Langston Hughes, by permission of Alfred A. Knopf, Inc.
**Cook's Mountains.** Used by permission of P.K. Page.
**Very Like a Whale** by Ogden Nash. Copyright 1934 by The Curtis Publishing Company. First appeared in *The Saturday Evening Post*. By permission of Little, Brown and Company.
**Erosion** by E.J. Pratt. Reprinted by permission of University of Toronto Press.
**The Immigrants** by Margaret Atwood. Reprinted from *The Journals of Susanna Moodie* by Margaret Atwood © Oxford University Press.
**The Shark** by E.J. Pratt. Reprinted by permission of University of Toronto Press.
**The Unnamed Lake** by F.G. Scott. Reprinted by permission of F.R. Scott.
**This is a Poem** by Paul Dutton by permission of the author © Paul Dutton 1975.
**Butterfly on Rock** by Irving Layton. From *Collected Poems of Irving*

**Ars Poetica** from *New and Collected Poems 1917-1976* by Archibald MacLeish. Copyright © 1976 by Archibald MacLeish. Reprinted by permission of Houghton Mifflin Company.
**Johnnie's Poem** by Alden Nowlan. From *Between Tears and Laughter* by Alden Nowlan © 1971 by Clarke, Irwin & Company Limited. Used by permission of Clarke Irwin (1983) Inc.
**Song 61** Douglas Barbour
**On the Value of Fantasies** by Elizabeth Brewster is reprinted from *Sometimes I Think of Moving* by permission of Oberon Press.
**The Future of Poetry in Canada** by Elizabeth Brewster. From *Sunrise North* by Elizabeth Brewster © 1972 by Clarke, Irwin & Company Limited. Used by permission of Clarke Irwin (1983) Inc.
**On The Other Side of the Poem** Rachel Korn
**The Bird by Patrick Lane** is reprinted by permission of the author with acknowledgement to Oxford University Press.
The photographs on the following pages are used by permission of Miller Services Limited: 8; 12; 22; 30—Peter Tasker, photographer; 44; 52; 60; 74; 86; 104; 118; 137; 144; 150—Richard Harrington, photographer; 162; 169—Gordon Beck, photographer; 178; 185; 189—Jürgen Mueller, photographer; 203—Marge Shackleton, photographer; 212; 226; 238—Gordon Beck, photographer.
The photographs on pages 95 and 111 are used by permission of Michael van Elsen.

Every effort has been made to obtain permission for copyright material used in this book, and to acknowledge all such indebtedness accurately. All errors and omissions called to our attention will be corrected in future printings.